Finding Shared Understanding between African Americans and the Police through Simulated Experiences

by John Pilz

DORRANCE
PUBLISHING CO
EST. 1920
PITTSBURGH, PENNSYLVANIA 15238

Dorrance Publishing Co
585 Alpha Drive
Pittsburgh, PA 15238
Visit our website at *www.dorrancebookstore.com*

ISBN: 978-1-4809-8606-0
eISBN: 978-1-4809-8588-9

"A culture could not survive long unless all of its members paid at-tention to at least a few of the same things".

-Mihaly Csikszentmihalyi

About the author

John J. Pilz is a 27+ year police officer in Minnesota. He has worked as a patrol deputy, investigator, narcotics detective, and K9 handler, 22 year SWAT operator and team leader, and as a sergeant in administration and patrol functions. He is a graduate of the FBI National Academy Session #222. This book is based on the research done as part of a doctoral dissertation. The original paper is titled, "Cultural understanding developed through simulated life experiences: A study of White police officers and African American citizens." John J. Pilz holds an Education Doctorate Degree in Leadership through Saint Mary's University of Minnesota, a Master's Degree in Police Leadership through the University of Saint Thomas in St. Paul, Minnesota, and a Bachelor's Degree through Metro State University in St. Paul, Minnesota. He has taught college criminal justice courses as an adjunct faculty member and cultural competency courses to law enforcement professionals. He is a high school baseball coach and father of six children.

Dedication

This book is dedicated to all of the men and women who wake up each day and proudly put on the uniform and the communities in which they serve.

Having the willingness to give your life to save a stranger takes a special person. We must be better, and we can. This research attempts to simultaneously better understand each other's culture. I have worn that uniform proudly and with honor for 27 years and wanted to give back new tools to help all of us work in a safer environment. Keep doing what is just and Godspeed!

This book is also dedicated to a group of people who have been treated as second-class citizens in the United States for far too long. African Americans have endured struggles since their beginning days in America. Through slow changes, their struggle for equality has not come easily. The purpose of this research was to show how we can come to more understanding of each other by walking in the other's shoes. These two cultures have different presumptions of who the other is and what the other does. Better understanding will ultimately lead to better relationships and less conflict in troubled times.

Acknowledgements

There are so many people to acknowledge for their assistance in my journey through this doctoral quest. To all of my classmates and professors at Saint Mary's University, your insights and shared knowledge have forever changed me. My eyes were opened to different worlds through the many classes and conversations. My committee has been especially insightful in opening my reality into new realities and I appreciate this. Dr. Wolfe, as my chair, your guidance and thought-provoking way of reaching me was essential. Dr. Pye, you always challenged my reality by explaining your reality. For this research to be successful, it needed your perspective. Dr. Mary Louise Wise, you added the perspectives from another background that help solidify this project. Dr. Booker Hodges, your background was something we needed to assure this research was properly examined through the eyes of a police officer.

There were also two special women (earth angels) in this journey who I cannot thank enough. The princess, Diana, and the smartest person in the room, Regina. You two have done more for me during this journey than any other people by volunteering countless hours of assistance both during classes and this dissertation. There are also numerous people who I work with that need to be acknowledged. Although there are too many to list, they also volunteered their time to assist me in creating the police videos, including my son, Nick. Your assistance helped accomplish this project. To my friend Al, thanks for your insight and assistance in this process as well. I also need to thank my father, Ned, who took those trips down to Wichita with me and assisted with the technical part of the project. There was no way I could have had this success without all of your help.

Laser Shot Inc. also partnered in this project. Through a reduced lease, this project was made possible. Scott Goodhart and Anderson Kith were always willing to help with equipment problems and video editing. Your efforts did not go unnoticed. Law Enforcement Labor Services also donated the funding to lease the equipment for this project. With countless other expenses, this offer was heart-felt and appreciated. To all of the business owners and administrators who helped me gain access to the venues to do the videos, you, too, contributed to this project and I appreciate your assistance. To all of my participants, I give my deepest gratitude. Although you did not always understand what the experience was measuring, I appreciate you volunteering to be a part of this study. Without you, this could not have come to fruition.

I save the most important for the end. Without the spiritual inspiration from the Lord above, I would have never started this journey. You alone know the mission I have been assigned, and I accept where it leads me. Thank you for your guidance in those frustrating and confusing times. Whenever I was in a rut, you brought me out.

Table of Contents

Introduction

Police officers in the United States have routinely been accused of racially-based policing tactics within the black community. Black community members have come to expect poor treatment from the police due to the combination of being black and living in distressed neighborhoods (Brunson, 2007, p. 85). Police officers, on the other hand, are sworn to protect the public they serve in a fair and impartial manner. This dichotomy of expectation has divided these two cultures of people from the days of slavery to the present. Recent events in Ferguson, Missouri, Staten Island, New York, and North Charleston, South Carolina have raised police distain as unarmed black men were killed by white police officers. A recent Gallup poll found the confidence in the police in the United States has fallen to its lowest level since 1993 (Jones, 2015, p.2). More recent shootings of black men in the summer of 2016 has strained relations further. Protests erupted across the United States after the shooting deaths of African-American men in St. Anthony, Minnesota and Baton Rouge, Louisiana.

During a peaceful protest in Dallas, Texas on July 7th, 2016, a lone gunman sniper opened fire on police officers working to protect the large crowd of protesters. Five officers were killed and two others were injured before the African-American gunman was stopped (Karimi, Shoichet, & Ellis, 2016, p. 1). Ten days later on July 17th, 2016, another attack on the police occurred in Baton Rouge, Louisiana when a gunman ambushed officers with a high-powered rifle. Three officers were fatally shot and three others were wounded. The African-American gunman was also killed in the shootout (Jansen, 2016, p. 1). Cultural misconceptions of who and where these two distinctly different cultures come from and what they are about demands further inquiry to end this cycle of unnecessary loss of life. This research delved into both cultures and attempted to find a way to create understanding and empathy, so both can better understand their cognitive perception of each other. Police officers in the United States are authorized by law to use deadly force under the following conditions based on *Tennessee v. Garner (1985)*: A crime has been committed and they believe the crime involved the threatened use or use of deadly force, or there is a substantial likelihood that if an apprehension is delayed, the suspect will cause death or serious bodily harm to another (Tennenbaum, 1994, p. 242-243). Wichita Police Policy 4.101 (2013) further states officers are justified to use deadly force if it is necessary to prevent resistance or escape from being defeated and such officer has probable cause to believe the suspect has committed or attempted to commit a felony involving death or great bodily harm or is attempting to escape by use of a deadly weapon, or otherwise indicates that such person will endanger human life or inflict great bodily harm unless arrested without delay (p. 1). This policy requires police officers to make split-second decisions, sometimes based on limited facts and time.

The media often reports information regarding officer-involved shootings based on limited facts before an investigation can be thoroughly conducted. Media reporting may contribute to distrust for the police within the African American community. As we have seen with recent officer-involved shootings across American, what was first reported to the media did not hold true during the investigation or trial in some cases. Police officers involved in deadly force situations are determined guilty by the public in many cases before they are given a fair investigation or trial, which every United States citizen is afforded by the Constitution. The public becomes angry with the police based on what is reported, and police officers become targets for events that they had nothing to do with.

To be fair, police officers who have crossed the line and committed crimes or made mistakes have also been found not guilty. There is a sense in the African-American culture that all an officer needs to do is say they were afraid for their safety to be vindicated in court. This creates more distrust and confusion for African-American citizens and people of color. The truth is an officer needs more than this for a not guilty verdict. However, there is a perception that this is not the case. The way the story gets portrayed in the media and social media can affect how the citizens understand the incident. This can also affect how this relationship continues to divide us. The truth is there have been people who wear the badge that are not ethical, honest, or righteous. These people do not deserve the honor of serving the community and should be stripped of their authority. However, the great majority of police officers in the United States took an oath to serve and protect, and they do this duty with great pride and honor.

Use of force incidents are not easy to traverse through. As we will see with the African-American participants in this study, there was an eye-opening effect on what use of force is like. Many participants commented on their surprise in how quickly things changed and became deadly. A decision occurs in split-second time, and the wrong decision can have profound consequences. There were participants who failed to shoot and were shot. There were participants who shot and likely would have been highly scrutinized in the media. The point is this is not as easy to make the "right" decision as the public believes. Regardless of the amount of training an officer receives, they are not prepared for every incident.

African-Americans having endured a long history of marginalization and unfair treatment by the police may presume each event is a progression of marginalization and racially-based policing. However, until there is a full understanding of how use of force is applied by the police, and until the police understand the history of marginalization, this dichotomy will surely persist. A thorough understanding of each "lived experience" is essential in breaking this barrier of understanding down. This "lived experience" event through simulation tested if emotional intelligence defined by Goleman (1998) as the ability to recognize one's own feelings and those of others, and the ability to manage emotions in our relationships and ourselves well (p. 317), can be accomplished through experiencing how the "other" lives in the world.

The white officers in this study had difficulty in many incidences in understanding what it is like to live marginalized on a routine basis. These officers also felt the effects of being treated like a second-class citizen. The results demonstrated empathy can be gained by experiencing another person's struggles through simulation. Some of these officers could not figure out what and why things were happening to them. Others became angry at how they were treated. There is a long history in this country of treating certain people and classes differently. These officers saw how this plays out through simulation.

This research study focused on creating cultural empathy and understanding between African-Americans and police officers. The setting for this study took place in Wichita, Kansas during 2017. There were 22 African-American civilians and 20 white police officers who participated in this study. The reason there were not any police officers of color allowed in this study was the fact they could have understood what it is like to feel marginalized at some point in their life. Most white people do not understand what being marginalized feels like. They live their lives with blinders on to racial and ethical mistreatment. They assume people are treated badly because they did something wrong. The truth is people are mistreated at times because of racial stereotyping or implicit bias.

Implicit bias is a "hot" topic in law enforcement today. Greenwald and Banaji (1995) define implicit bias as unconscious attitudes, both negative and positive, towards other people, groups, or ideas (p. 5). All people have implicit bias, but do they recognize it and act on it? Although implicit biases can be developed and altered throughout a person's life, these negative biases can affect how a person acts towards another person or group. If a police officer has implicit bias towards a group of people (African-Americans, Hispanics, gays or lesbians, Muslims, ect.), she/he may act differently than they would towards a group or person if they do not have this bias. This can affect how an officer performs their job and play a role in their discretion to issue a citation or jail a person. The key is to understand these biases, acknowledge they exist, and consciously avoid allowing them to effect the way an officer performs his/her job.

Quantitative research was not chosen as a method to collect data for this study because it would not reach the feelings people experience in the deep meaningful way that can be achieved through in-depth qualitative means. Quantitative research can use surveys, which give value to participant's thoughts to each question with a number ranking. African-Americans and police officers could not express their deeply-held feelings nor convey empathy through the use of a Likert-type scale to gain in-depth understanding of how their experience effected their understanding of police use of force or being marginalized. Yin (2011) contends qualitative research may help explain human social behavior and represents the views and perspectives of participants (p. 6-7). Fraenkel, Wallen, and Hyun (2012) posit qualitative data primarily involves words, whereas quantitative data primarily deals with numbers. Based on their belief that facts and feelings can be separate, quantitative researchers base their world on a single reality of facts that can be discovered (p. 7).

This research study holds limitations as well. As with most qualitative studies, this research was done with a small sample size from both cultures. Results cannot be construed as indicative of all major metropolitan police forces within the United States. Assessment of personal views from inter-actions with this sample of participants cannot be generalized as over-all po-lice bias or racism. Police officers who hold such thoughts may not have chosen to participate in this research study. African-Americans who distrust the police also may have avoided participating in this research study. Results reflected in this study should be understood as a very small portion of the general population's understanding of marginalization and police use of force. Data gathered from this study investigated commonly used phrases and pat-terns in emotional changes through words between pre-post interviews. This data should not be construed to reflect general assumptions based on these sample sizes.

The use of simulation cannot duplicate "real life" use of force situations nor the feeling of being marginalized. The instrument used for this investiga-tion was Laser Shot Inc. simulated experiences. Laser Shot Inc. is one of many simulation products on the market, but it is not validated as being the best simulation equipment available for this type of research study. For this reason, the results from this study may not be the same as they would with a different simulator to experience what cultural empathy and understanding feels like. Time constraints only allowed this researcher to evaluate reactions and changes in understanding due to distance and requirements for this research. Other studies with access to more participants and time may extract different results. Although in-depth qualitative interviews may extract more data on how participants feel before and after this experience, self-reporting on the experience may contain biased views and opinions. This researcher could not control for intentional or unintentional bias in self-reported data.

Another limitation of this study was once a few officers had finished the experiment, they were asked to keep the scenarios confidential until the study was completed. However, the researcher's experience with police culture allows insight into the communicative nature of the profession, therefore to maintain experimental integrity, all 20 experiments were conducted in a short time span. Officers who understood what the scenarios were meant to measure may have manipulated their personal feelings and skewed the data. Although there was the potential for the African-American participants to all talk about their experience with each other, this was less likely as the participants may not have known each other and therefore were less likely to be in situations where long conversations were probable.

A final limitation to this study was the researcher is a member of one of the cultures. The researcher is a 27 year veteran police officer. While it was challenging to avoid biased interpretations, the researcher let the participants' words speak for them in this research. Non-leading questions were asked, and clarifying follow-up questions did not change the participants' views.

Gaining access and getting cooperation from 20 police officers and 20 African-American participants had the potential to be complicated. Gaining access to a large metropolitan police department was a complication in and of itself. There are few progressive leaders in police departments who are willing to assist researchers for fear of possible controversial results. Having been a police officer for 27 years allowed some access and trust from fellow officers in this culture, however, re-assuring cynical veteran officers that by participating their statements and actions would remain anonymous and confidential was challenging. As discussed in chapter four, officers have a culture that is skeptical of outsiders. It was assumed 20 police officers would be willing volunteer participants in this study and take the experiment through simulation seriously. It was also assumed that there were more than 20 African-Americans in this large city that would be willing to better understand police use of force and participate in this research.

Assumptions are things taken for granted and not tested or checked (Fraenkel et al., 2012, p. 17). Assumptions for this study dealt with understanding cultural differences through simulated experiences of another culture. It was assumed these experiences would create better understanding and empathy towards the other culture. It was also assumed the principal researcher could avoid bias and misleading questions due to his extensive police background. A prewritten format of participant questions was written and adhered to during the interview process. All statements were audio recorded with participant permission to reduce researcher bias.

Brunson (2007) posits future research should address personal and indirect experiences to further emphasize citizens' assessments of the police, which require comprehensive methods that can allow better understanding of the police, which can ultimately shape their perceptions (p. 96). The same can be said for police officers understanding African-Americans' lived experience of marginalization to develop better understanding and build collaborative relationships. The tension between the police and African-Americans has become more apparent in recent years and understanding each other's lived experience in a different forum could produce empathy and understanding for future collaboration. Lee (2016) interviewed African-American police officers for their views of living in both worlds of this dichotomy. One Chicago officer who has always been troubled by the lack of empathy some white colleagues show towards the black residents they serve during his 22-year career in police work stated, "I wouldn't say that all of the white officers, or even the average one, has no empathy. But I would say a lot of them don't have any empathy, and at times, they don't even understand that they don't. But in the things that they say, you see it" (p. 4).

There has been an increase in dissatisfaction with the police from the African-American communities due to many recently publicized officer involved use of force incidents on unarmed African-Americans in the United States. Tensions have led to riots and ambush attacks on police officers related to these incidents. African-Americans feel an increased outrage of being racially profiled based on the color of their skin, and police officers feel general hatred upon them from the actions of a few police officers, which is not reflective of their actions as a police officer. Without intervention, tensions will surely rise, causing more unnecessary deaths to both groups. This problem needed to be addressed to create dialogue and training with both groups to eliminate tensions and unnecessary future deaths.

From Eric Garner in New York City, to Michael Brown in Ferguson, Missouri in 2014. Walter Scott in North Charleston, North Carolina in 2015, to Keith Lamar Scott in Tulsa, Oklahoma in 2016, this dichotomy has risen to higher stakes. From four officers in Lakeland, Washington being ambushed and killed while meeting for breakfast in 2009 to NYPD officers Ramos and Liu being ambushed and killed while sitting in their police squad in 2014. Five Dallas officers while protecting peaceful demonstrators lose their lives in an ambush in July 2016, and just ten days later, three Baton Rouge officers lost their lives in an ambush at the hands of a former marine. Many others not mentioned in this short period of time have also needlessly lost their life during this period as well. This dichotomy is getting more luminous each day in America, and change must come ahead of substantial more life-loss.

In order to better understand these two cultures, it is necessary to see who they are and how they have evolved. For this reason, the following chapters will better articulate their history to better understand their culture. It is necessary to understand this before understanding how this has affected the current state between the police and African-American cultures.

A Summary of African-American History

Washington (1910) stated the first African-American slaves arrived as early as 1619 in Jamestown, Virginia, however, it was nearly a half century later before African-Americans made up large numbers in the southern colonies (p. 125). The first American census was done in 1790. At this time, there were nearly 700,000 slaves in America. The state of Virginia had nearly 40% of the slaves at this time totaling nearly 300,000 (Walker, 1998, p. 23). African-Americans endured brutal living conditions, including beatings, lynching, and poor living conditions in America. These slaves lived this existence as best as they could. They attempted to negotiate with their masters for more autonomy or tried to strike deals for material improvements. For most who lived under the heavy hand of slavery, material well-being, or autonomy were the goals. Freedom was an idea beyond reach (Klooster, 2014, p. 403). Controlling the slaves was left to the masters who were given full authority of both slaves and servants and were empowered by the criminal justice system and courts (Walker, 1998, p. 24). A 1669 Virginia statute contended it was not a felony for a master to kill a stubborn African-American slave because the slave was considered property (Feagin, 2013, p. 47).

Agriculture was the primary source of money and wealth in America in her early years. The south needed workers for the sugar plantations in Louisiana, cotton plantations in Alabama, rice plantations in South Carolina, and tobacco plantations in Virginia (Goffe, 2011, p. 74). In South Carolina in the later part of the seventeenth century, rice production became a lucrative crop in both America and Europe. The solution to South Carolina's workforce shortage was to import tens of thousands of African captives to the colony to labor in the rice fields (Kyles, 2008, p. 500-501). With the ever increasing amount of slaves in the colonies, the need for controlling the slaves became more prevalent. Slave patrols were established to maintain control of the slaves. These slave patrols were first established by colonial leaders in 1686 (Kyles, 2008, p. 501). In the state of Virginia, for example, more than 130 slave statutes were enacted between 1689 and 1865. The U.S. legal system passed Fugitive Slave laws through Congress in 1789 and 1850 to strengthen control over the large slave populations (Durr, 2015, p. 874).

Resistance to the oppressive nature of slavery ensued during the years of slavery. On September 9th, 1739 in the early morning hours, an organized revolt started. This revolt began on the western branch of the Stono River in St. Paul's Parish South Carolina. With a group of approximately 20 men under the command of a slave named Jemmy, they seized weapons and gunpowder from a local store after decapitating the two storekeepers. This group made its way towards Georgia, killing the whites who confronted them. Some Africans joined the group voluntarily, while others were forced to join (Kyles, 2008, p. 504). As the group proceeded, they would stop to dance, sing, and beat drums. After gaining in size to approximately 90, they were met by a militia, which dispersed the group leaving some dead. The rebellion was eventually stopped by mounted troops nearly a week later after several battles (Thornton, 1991, p. 11).

In 1831, a slave by the name of Nat Turner led one of the largest slave revolts in U.S. history. Nat Turner spent his entire life as a slave from 1800-1831 in Southampton, Virginia. Turner was a religious figure in the slave community, allowing him authority over other slaves. Over the course of the 40-hour revolt, Turner amassed between 60 and 80 slaves, and this group killed between 55 and 65 slaveholders (Drexler-Dreis, 2014, p. 230-231).

Between the Revolutionary and Civil Wars, property laws emphasized the protection of individual rights. These rights, however, were only afforded to white men with resources to support dependents (Edwards, 2002, p. 389). Southern states through their appellate decisions and statutes not only denied rights to individual slaves, but also restricted the civil and political rights of free black people and poor white men along with all women (Edwards, 2002, p. 368). In 1857, the Supreme Court made a ruling in *Dred Scott v. Sandford*.

This case involved Scott, a slave who was transferred to Illinois, a non-slave state, from Missouri, a slave state by his army surgeon master. Scott argued he should now be free to the Supreme Court. The court, however, ruled that Scott had no right to bring the case to court because he was not a "citizen" within the Constitution. According to Chief Justice Taney, neither free blacks nor slaves could ever be a part of the American political community (Pollak, 2005, p. 30-31). Chief Justice Taney also inferred African-Americans were inherently inferior to whites and therefore could be justifiably subjugated. The first article of the Constitution declared at the time that when states were determining populations, "all other persons" were to be counted as three fifths of a person. This was clearly directed towards slaves (Goff, Eberhardt, Williams, & Jackson, 2008, p. 292). Edwards (2002) points out that state and national governments of the time were considered weak, so much authority was delegated to the local jurisdictions (p. 369). On April 12th, 1861, war was declared between the North and South over the slavery issue. The South chose secession over ending slavery. With the assistance of approximately 200,000 African-Americans, the Union won the Civil War paying a high price with approximately 40,000 African-American casualties (Goffe, 2011, p. 75). On April 9th, 1865, the Civil War ended. The Reconstruction Era thus began.

Four million African-American slaves were emancipated after the Civil War ended. These former slaves, however, were set free without job skills, education, and experience in public life to lead them in their new-found freedom. Tens of thousands of former slaves were obligated to work as sharecroppers or as tenants for their former slave masters for low wages, or in some cases, no wage at all in the decades that followed the war. The standard of living was only a slight notch above that of slavery. The federal government assistance, which was intended to assist the former slaves' transition into their newly found freedom, disappeared within a decade of the end of the Civil War, leaving former slaves to fend for themselves (Madigan, 2001, p. 9).

After the Civil War ended, the Congress and President quickly added three amendments to the U. S. Constitution. The Thirteenth Amendment was added in 1865, which abolished slavery. The Fourteenth Amendment was added in 1868, which gave citizenship to all persons born or naturalized in the

United States. This added amendment overruled the Dred Scott Supreme Court decision of 1857. The Fifteenth Amendment was then added in 1870, giving all male African-Americans the right to vote (Pollak, 2005, p. 32). In 1875, the federal government passed the Civil Rights Act of which Congress was seeking to enforce the new amendments, which required all people to be served at public inns, conveyances on land or water, theaters, and other public places regardless of their race (Pollak, 2005, p. 33).

With the end of slavery, new prejudices, laws, and suffrage started for the African-Americans particularly in the American south. Peonage, convict leasing, and Jim Crow laws became the new norm for African-Americans living in the south. Washington (1910) contended white people in the south were convinced both races were better off having their own preachers and teachers and school and church matters should be managed among themselves (p. 131). Post-Civil War African-American communities were first established around little churches. At the time, the church was the center through which African-American life revolved. In the beginning of reconstruction, it was the only distinctive black institution in existence (Washington, 1912, p. 83). Du Bois (1903) contends that the churches of the south are governments of men. In the south, nearly every American negro is a church member. Every person must have a social center, and for the southern African-American, it is the negro church (p. 91). In the early years, support for the African-American churches were aligned with the Baptist or Methodist denominations (Washington, 1912, p. 83).

Struggles ensued for the African-Americans living in the south. Du Bois (1903) documents that southern legislatures were unwilling to allow freed African-American slaves to the polls and suggested there was not a single white man in the south who did not view emancipation as a crime (p. 21). Without the ability to vote, Du Bois (1903) contends the African-Americans will never be able to be free. "The ballot, which before he had looked upon as a visible sign of freedom, he now regarded as the chief means of gaining and perfecting the liberty with which was had partially endowed him" (p. 7). After the Civil War, the government seized property from the former Confederate states and gave it to freed African-Americans. However, working the land required tools, which were not afforded to them. White merchants used this as an opportunity to exploit the African-Americans. Mortgages were written to allow these African-Americans to purchase food, clothing, tools, and supplies, which became payable when the crops were harvested. Interest was added to these mortgages, causing the African-Americans to pay more for everything they purchased. When the cotton prices were up, African-Americans could gain profits from their labor. Merchants always encouraged the African-Americans to purchase more when the prices were up and never to save their gains. When cotton rose ten cents one fall, a shrewd merchant sold a thousand buggies in one season, mostly to black men (Du Bois, 1903, p. 70). In the year 1898, cotton prices were low and 300 tenant families in one Georgia county found themselves in debt at the end of the season. Payments for these debts were heartless when merchants came to collect and took everything of value from the tenant families. These former slaves became slaves again to their debt (Du Bois, 1903, p. 71).

Slavery did not disappear in all of the South in a pure sense. Strict instructions came out of Washington D.C. that African-Americans were free to choose their employers with no fixed wage rates and no peonage or forced labor was allowed (Du Bois, 1903, p. 17). However, in many Gulf states, especially Mississippi, Louisiana, and Arkansas, there were plantations in the backcountry districts still using forced laborers. This was particularly true where the farmers were composed of a more ignorant class of poor whites, and the African-Americans were beyond the reach of schools or other advancing blacks (Du Bois, 1903, p. 71).

African-American scholars of the early 1900's, Du Bois (1903) and Washington (1911) agreed the best way for the former slaves to advance was through education. However, the cost of survival in the fields required children to work most of the year. Washington (1911) argued, "It is by means of practical education that the negro is to be developed and made a useful citizen" (p. 177). Du Bois (1903) contends that one out of every five dollars is spent on public education in the state of Georgia for African-American schools. The other four are spent on white schools (p. 85).

Another continued problem for African-Americans in the post-Civil War era was the increased crime, punishment, and prejudice for African-Americans.

Du Bois (1903) illustrated that a black stranger in Baker County, Georgia was liable to be stopped anywhere on the public highway and be required to state his business to the satisfaction of any white interrogator. If he fails or seems too independent or "sassy," he may be arrested. This in turn could lead to peonage of the arrested male (p. 72). Other "crimes" were adopted by southern states, such as vagrancy, which made it a crime to not work. These crimes were applied to blacks in most cases, and the penalty was usually convict leasing imposed by state laws to allow county governments to lease prisoners to plantation owners for labor, which was done for little or no pay (Alexander, 2011, p. 28). Du Bois (1903) documents this growing problem in the south by articulating the "stockades" or county prison is full of what white people call black criminals, and black folks complain that only colored boys go to jail. Not because they are guilty but because the state needs criminals for income from forced labor (p. 60).

From 1865 to 1870, Joseph E. Brown, chief justice of the Supreme Court in Georgia, used African-American men convicted under America's racist laws to work in his coal mines, making him a large fortune (Cush, 2013, p. 73). This type of peonage is today referred to as institutional capital in America. The abuse of black prisoners for precisely this purpose advanced Judge Brown, along with his state's economic interest (Cush, 2013, p. 74). Today, the United States is seeing an explosion of incarceration, especially in the black community. New private prisons have been erected, and they crave more people to gain financially. According to Aman and Greenhouse (2014), the growth in jails and prisons was not due to general criminal activity, rather, this was due to expanded criminalization, in particular drug crimes, along with so-called three-strike laws (p. 377). Today, these private prisons supply labor to private businesses for pennies on the dollar.

Not all things were going wrong for the African-Americans during the Reconstruction Era. The first African-American bank was established in the late 1880's. By the early 1910's, there were over 60 African-American owned banks in the United States (Washington, 1912, p. 82). African-American Universities were also being built during this period, allowing African-Americans the ability to gain an advanced education. George L. White led a group of four African-American boys and five girl-women, the Fisk Jubilee Singers, around the country and as far away as Ireland, Switzerland and Holland to sing slave songs starting in 1871. They brought back 150,000 dollars to fund Fisk University after seven years of performing (Du Bois, 1903, p. 118).

Following Peonage and convict leasing, African-Americans were subjected to the Jim Crow Era. The term Jim Crow came from a minstrel character and was regarded as the permanent system of racial control (Alexander, 2011, p. 35). The Jim Crow Era and new laws of segregation spread rapidly in the Southern states in the 1880's and 1890's (Pollak, 2005, p. 35). The U. S. Supreme Court decision of *Plessy v. Ferguson* made it legal to have "separate but equal" treatment determining where African-Americans were allowed to go (Sigelman & Welch, 1991, p. 18). In 1890, Louisiana enacted a statute requiring all black and white railroad passengers be seated in separate cars with criminal penalties for violators. There was an exception for African-American nurses attending to white children (Pollak, 2005, p. 35). In the middle of the 1800's into the 1900's, African-Americans were portrayed in the newspapers and magazines in highly racist fashion. Cartoons depicted African-Americans as having "ugly" (to whites), negative physical characteristics, such as distinctive hair, lips, skin, and odor. Black women were stereotyped as sexually promiscuous, and black men were labelled "Zip Coon" dandies (Feagin, 2013, p. 74). Goff et al. (2008) points out early movies, such as King Kong, deliberately depicted the "beauty" as white and the "beast" as black (p. 293). Feagin (2013) contends the constant media and minstrel portrayals of African-Americans helped maintain negative images for the white racial frame (p. 76). The white frame was bombarded with stereotyping about African-American physical deficiencies, low intelligence, and cultural inferiority. These negative attacks were embraced by leading politicians, business leaders, and social and physical scientists. Even President Calvin Coolidge argued in a popular magazine that biological laws stipulate certain divergent people will not mix or blend (Feagin, 2013, p. 83).

As early as 1909, seeing a growing problem among the separation of races, black and white intellectuals and philanthropists got together and formed the National Association for the Advancement of Colored People (NAACP). The only original black leader of this organization was W. E. B. Du Bois (Sigelman & Welch, 1991, p. 18-19). Sigelman and Welch (1991) contend the early mission of the NAACP was concentrated on bringing greater racial equality through education and legal action. There were continued acts of lynching occurring approximately eight times a year in the first decade of the 1900's, however, it became a central focus early on with the NAACP (p. 19).

In late May 1921, Tulsa, Oklahoma became the site of one of the worst "race riots" in American history. An African-American shoeshine boy named Dick Rowland was alleged to have assaulted a white girl in an elevator in the Drexel Building in downtown Tulsa. The local newspaper, the *Tulsa Tribune*, printed the story on May 31st, 1921 in a way that portrayed the white girl as an upstanding innocent victim and Rowland as an aggressive criminal negro. The original copy of this newspaper was only a couple hundred copies before the newspaper recanted the editorial, however, emotions brewed high after word circulated throughout Tulsa. The headline of this story originally said: "To lynch negro tonight" (Madigan, 2001, p. 45-46). The aftermath of this *Tribune* story created intense emotions with the African-Americans in their community of Greenwood over this potential lynching. Greenwood was considered one of the most successful African-American stories where black doctors, lawyers, and businessmen thrived. Greenwood was also a place where proud World War One veteran soldiers lived, and black Tulsa in their mind would not allow any lynching of African-Americans (Madigan, 2001, p. 170).

While white crowds grew at the sheriff's office demanding the sheriff turn over Dick Rowland, word spread throughout Greenwood. A group of black leaders went to the courthouse at around nine o'clock to protect Dick Rowland from the white mob. After being reassured by Sheriff McCullough that Rowland would be safe with him, the group left back to Greenwood. However, in a night filled with rumors, word circulated that the white mob had assaulted the courthouse and were trying to get Rowland. Approximately 75 armed African-Americans went back to the courthouse around 10:15 PM to save Rowland. Once at the courthouse, they observed the white mob had not gained access to the courthouse. However, an old white man confronted an African-American World War One veteran who had a pistol and demanded the African-American give him his pistol. A struggle ensued and shots were fired. Thus, starting the "Tulsa Riots" on May 31st, 1921 (Madigan, 2001, p. 101-103).

At dawn on June 1st, 1921 after a night of gun battles between the thousands of whites and hundreds of blacks, the Tulsa whites began their invasion into Greenwood. whites systematically burned and looted their way through Greenwood that day. Kerosene or gasoline was dumped in every building before being put to the torch. Fire crews were prohibited from saving the structures by an armed white mob (Madigan, 2001, p. 120). Greenwood, which was home to some 15,000 African-Americans, laid in ruins by the end of the day on June 1st, 1921. Hundreds of African-Americans were killed, and thousands fled their homes or were captured and detained (Madigan, 2001, p. 219).

Madigan (2001) points out two key factors that were swelling racial emotions within the white community. The book, *The Clansman*, written by Dixon became a national best seller. This book depicted African-Americans as having animal characteristics and animal odor. Obsessed by rape, Dixon portrayed African-American men as eagerly wanting to rape white women and characterized the Civil War as the North raping the South. A film called *Birth of a Nation* also appeared to glamorize the Ku Klux Klan as heroes who rescue a young white girl from a crazed black renegade named Gus (p. 60-61). In Tulsa, Oklahoma, the wealth and success of African-Americans also contributed to the white rage and racially charged emotions, which caused such destruction.

After the Great Depression ended, financial experts of the time concluded poor real estate investments were partially to blame for the financial collapse. To deal with this issue, the federal government created banking standards designed to give the best mortgages and loans in areas where the least amount of poor and minorities lived. Areas were given ratings to determine if the location was ineligible or a cautious one. This became known as "redlining" (Woods, 2012, p. 1038). Fullilove and Wallace (2011) highlight the practice of redlining was instituted by the Home Owners Loan Corporation (HOLC) in 1937 to steer investment away from risky areas. These areas were articulated as places with older buildings and non-white residents. The presence of one African-American family in the area was given the worst rating. This process caused a foundation for white flight (p. 382). Woods (2012) claims the HOLC did not create racial and economic bias, however, it did help nationalize its practice (p. 1038). Race, ethnicity, and class became so influencing when a neighborhood's desirability was assessed that these factors surpassed all other appraisal considerations. During a period in history that the government was expanding the American dream to millions of white middle-class citizens, African-Americans and other minorities were being barred from full access to home ownership and trapped in inhabitable and inadequate spaces (Woods, 2012, p. 1039).

In 1949, the federal Housing Act authorized the government to legally seize property through the power of eminent domain in areas, which it determined were less appealing. The land was cleared and re-sold at reduced pricing to developers for new "higher" uses. The term used for this process was urban renewal. Large areas of land were cleared for the construction of cultural centers, housing projects, universities, and other developments. The areas most affected by this process were in African-American neighborhoods. Nearly three-quarters of the inhabitants included in this process were African-American (Fullilove & Wallace, 2011, p. 382).

During the late 1950's and early 1960's, African-Americans began to mobilize against every aspect of legal segregation. In 1950, the Supreme Court ruled that Oklahoma had to desegregate its law school in the case of *McLaurin v. Oklahoma* (Alexander, 2011, p. 36). The 1954 U. S. Supreme court decision of *Brown v. The Board of Education* held that equal public education could not be separated by ethnicity. This ruling started a series of civil disobediences to end legal segregation and make equal treatment for all races (Sigelman & Welch, 1991, p. 19-20). The 1960's brought the Civil Rights movement, challenging deeply entrenched inequality, including criminal justice discrimination (Walker, 1998, p. 194). New African-American leaders emerged, like Dr. Martin Luther King Jr. and Malcolm X to advocate for change. With the continued pressure exerted by African-Americans, the Civil Rights Act of 1964 was passed. The Civil Rights Act opened the door to African-Americans for equal protection. It overturned the doctrine of "separate but equal" in all public places and barred discrimination in employment, housing, and education. The

1965 Voting Rights Act made it a crime to interfere with a person's right to vote, and authorized federal officials to register voters (Sigelman & Welch, 1991, p. 20-21). Walker (1998) argues the transformation of the southern states from the mid-1960's into the mid-1970's was the most dramatic change in the history of American criminal justice (p. 194).

With all of the transition into the new American order, the rise of the Ku Klux Klan reasserted itself as a powerful and feared threat to African-Americans in the South. Castrations, killings, and bombings of African-American churches and homes became more prevalent. Anyone speaking up in favor of equal rights became a target. NAACP leaders were pistol-whipped, beaten, and shot (Alexander, 2011, p. 37).

This time period in American history also had another ominous side. Race riots erupted during this period in major U. S. cities, causing millions of dollars in damage, many injuries, and deaths and strained relations between the races. On July 16th, 1964, a white, off-duty New York City police officer shot and killed a 15-year-old African-American. Two nights later, civil rights protesters ascended on the 28th precinct headquarters. When the police tried to break-up the crowd, a riot ensued. Over the next few weeks, riots broke out in Rochester, Philadelphia, and Jersey City. In 1965, the Watts community of Los Angeles erupted in a riot, lasting six days, taking 34 lives, and a thousand injuries. In 1966 and 1967, riots occurred in Chicago, Cleveland, San Francisco, Atlanta, along with at least 40 other American cities. In 1967, the violence and destruction was worse. Newark, New Jersey saw $10 million in damages, and 23 people dead over a five-day period. In Detroit, Michigan, 43 people died and $40 million of damage was recorded in a riot that lasted nearly one week (Walker, 1998, p. 196).

The 1980's brought new forms of discrimination to African-Americans in the United States. Inequalities in enforcement of laws was accelerated as a result of President Reagan's "war on drugs" (Feagin, 2013, p. 153). Between 1980 and 1984, federal law enforcement agencies' budgets soared. FBI, Department of Defense antidrug allocations, and DEA budgets rose ten-fold at times to increase enforcement of the new federal drug laws (Alexander, 2011, p. 49). In 1987, new federal sentencing guidelines went into effect. These new guidelines were designed to increase severity of punishment for drug offenders. As a result of these new guidelines, federal prisoner rates soared in numbers. The most notorious feature of these new laws was the 100 to one penalties for cocaine. Possession of one gram of crack was equivalent to 100 grams of powder cocaine. During the mid-1980's, crack was the drug of choice for African-Americans, and powder cocaine was the choice of whites (Walker, 1998, p. 220). Crack cocaine arrived in 1985. It was sold at low cost in rock form, which was then smoked. This opened new markets to the poor and young people. International cartels imported the drugs, and national gang networks distributed the drugs at the neighborhood level. Local drug gangs proceeded to take over some poor neighborhoods, causing urban turf wars, which dramatically increased the murder rate in cities (Walker, 1998, p. 228).

As a result of the increases in drug violations and gang violence, incarcerations soared. In 1995, the Sentencing Project found that 30% of African-American men between 20-29 years of age were in the hands of the criminal justice system either through incarceration, parole, or probation on any given day (Walker, 1998, p. 230). The result of these new enforcement actions deemed felonies has left an unprecedented escalation in criminal punishment in the United States, while simultaneously taking the voting rights away from millions of African-Americans (Peffley & Hurwitz, 2010, p. 150).

The landscape changed for race relations with the videotaped 1991 beating of Rodney King by Los Angeles police officers and the not guilty verdict of hall of fame NFL running back O. J. Simpson in 1995. On March 3rd, 1991, Rodney King, an African-American who was on parole and had been convicted of second-degree robbery, led California Highway Patrol officers on a high-speed chase on a San Fernando Valley freeway. When he finally stopped, the intoxicated King initially resisted and was brought down to his knees by police officers. While still rolling on the ground, King was subsequently beaten, kicked, and struck with police batons some 56 times. This obvious extreme excessive use of police force was captured on video by an amateur photographer who sold the tape to a Los Angeles television station. The continual playing of the video induced outrage by the entire community but specifically the African-American community who saw this as an act of racism. Three officers and a sergeant were charged with felonies, including assault with a deadly weapon. However, on April 29th, 1992, the jury returned a verdict of not guilty on the serious charges and failed to reach a verdict on the lesser charge of filing a false police report. At 5:30 PM that evening, violence and rioting broke out in Los Angeles, which lasted until May 2nd. In all, 38 people died, 1,200 people were injured, 3,000 arrested, 1,500 buildings were set on fire, and $500 million in property damage was done (Miller, 2001, p. 193-195).

The OJ Simpson not guilty verdict caused an opposite effect. Many African-Americans were jubilant with the verdict while whites were dumbfounded. This experience allowed many whites for the first time to experience collectively what they perceived as misconduct by the criminal justice system. Something African-Americans experience on a day-to-day basis (Stewart, 1995, p. 44). The prosecutor in this case chose to pick a mostly African-American female jury on the belief that African-American women are more experienced in domestic violence and would be more sympathetic to the prosecution (Stewart, 1995, p. 43). Stewart (1995) explains this had a negative effect amongst many white Americans who saw this as evidence that African-Americans were intellectually inferior (p. 44).

Peffley and Hurwitz (2010) contend that public reactions to highly publicized cases, such as these constitute "flashpoints" in the racial divide (p. 112). Peffley and Hurwitz point out that brutality and racial profiling are commonplace to many African-Americans, thus African-Americans as a group are likely to view confrontations with the police as another instance of discrimination (p. 121). Washington (1911) points out that throughout history, African-Americans have had difficulty dealing with the law and the police because African-Americans fresh out of slavery have not been able to dis-associate law from slavery (p. 176). The police are sometimes viewed as the enforcer of the laws aimed at keeping African-Americans as second-class citizens. This may also contribute to African-Americans reluctance to speak with the police when crimes occur. Although there may be witnesses to crimes in the black community, citizen's lack of trust of the police may cause these people to decide not to help them. This confuses the police and the public when an innocent person is murdered and no one will assist the police in finding the killer. Looking at this in another way, when the police commit crimes and their partners are unwilling to turn them in, is there a difference? As will be discussed later, when the police protect "bad" cops, is this any different than citizens protecting criminals? In this case, two wrongs do not make a right.

Johnson (2008) postulates under the conflict model that punitive crime policies are rooted in blacks' and whites' social structure. Whites, the dominant group, support punitive policies which are associated with the status quo. African-Americans believe the justice system is biased towards them, thus they support less tempered punitive policies (p. 199). In a research study with 978 non-Hispanic whites and 1,010 non-Hispanic blacks living in the U.S., Johnson (2008) found the majority of whites were in favor of punitive sanctions to charge juvenile violent crime suspects in adult courts, compared to a smaller amount of black respondents. Less than half of the black respondents thought penalties were "too light" for violent criminal offenders, yet two thirds of whites felt penalties were "too light" (p. 202). Johnson (2008) noted that blacks were significantly less punitive when they had a friend or relative incarcerated or when they perceived racial bias in the criminal justice system than their counterparts (p. 202). Johnson (2008) concluded that the legitimacy of the criminal justice system has serious questions when there is widespread mistrust and a lack of confidence by a large portion of the community (p. 205).

Hagan and Albonetti (1982) conducted a study with 1,049 respondents where the head of household was known to be employed and 59 respondents where the head of household was known to be unemployed, not retired, a student, or housewife (p.333). Results from this study produced three major findings: (1) criminal injustice is perceived to be considerably more likely by more African-Americans than whites; (2) regardless of race, perceived criminal injustice is more likely from members of the surplus population than members of other classes; (3) the white professional managerial class is more likely to not hold a perception of criminal injustice compared to the same class of other races. The perception of criminal injustice was also more pronounced in the metropolitan centers compared to other parts of the nation (p. 352).

There have been numerous Department of Justice (DOJ) investigations over the last few decades into police departments across the United States. In a March 2015 in a DOJ investigative report into the Ferguson, Missouri Police Department after the shooting of an unarmed African-American teenager and riots causing millions of dollars in losses found numerous discriminatory practices by both the police and the city leaders. African-Americans made up 67% of the population in Ferguson, Missouri, however, they accounted for 85% of the traffic stops conducted by the police. African-Americans in Ferguson received 90% of the traffic citations, and 93% of arrests from 2012 to 2014 (DOJ, 2015, p. 62). The DOJ (2015) obtained numerous documents of police malfeasance, including the use of a canine on an unarmed 14-year-old African-American boy who was trespassing in an abandoned house. Although the police were dispatched to a burglary in progress, the facts showed this to be merely a trespassing offense (p. 32). The DOJ (2015) also reported officers routinely violated the Fourth Amendment by stopping and searching individuals without reasonable suspicion, making arrests without probable cause, and using unreasonable force. These police practices were shaped by the city of Ferguson's pressure to raise revenue (p. 15).

Living African American

From the time of slavery to the present day, African-Americans have held on to a distinct culture. This culture has evolved from African tradition, living as slaves, being set free, and living with marginalized citizenry. Peterson and Krivo (2010) contend privileged racial groups have much to lose from racial equality. Maintaining the status quo is essential in preserving the benefits of the dominant race. Those in subordinate groups lack the power to change their position in the system (p. 21). According to Peterson and Krivo (2010), there is a clear racial-spatial divide in the United States. Inequality in social and economic power and circumstances in society combined with segregated and unequal living locations across major racial and ethnic groups of people. This racial-spatial divide causes African-Americans to hold the least amount of power and the most disadvantage (p. 32). Disadvantaged neighborhoods have heightened crime rates for two reasons: First, criminal behavior is encouraged where disadvantage surrounds people, and second, disadvantaged neighborhoods lack the social control mechanisms which normally discourage criminal involvement (Peterson & Krivo, 2010, p. 33-34). Peterson and Krivo (2010) contend through their research that 85% of all African-American neighborhoods are extremely disadvantaged. Many African-Americans have few options to leave these neighborhoods; in a sense, they are confined to living in African-American parts of the city (p. 62-63).

Peterson and Krivo (2010) argue that greater violence occurs in cities that are segregated. A stronger manufacturing base lowers neighborhood violence. Stable, well-paying jobs reduces violence in all neighborhoods. Neighborhoods where more residential loans are gained showing external investment into communities causes a universal drop in both violent and property crimes

(p. 118-119). American cities are more segregated than other parts of the world. Harris (1999) assessed housing prices fell at least 16% when the population of the neighborhood has at least 10% black residents. Harris (1999) contends housing in neighborhoods with large African-Americans residents are less valuable because people prefer affluent, well-educated neighbors, and these traits are more common among whites (p. 476). Massey, Gross, and Shibuya (1994) claim the concentration of poor people in neighborhoods leads to a concentration of crime, violence, educational failure, family disruption, and welfare dependency (p. 426). Due to racial segregation, blacks who are not poor have a hard time escaping poor neighborhoods. This racial segregation isolates African-Americans economically and socially, contributing to the accumulation of poverty in black neighborhoods (Massey et. al, 1994, p. 443). South and Crowder (1998) postulate very few African-Americans move from a predominantly black neighborhood into a predominantly white neighborhood. African-Americans have a high rate of moving out of white neighborhoods and a low rate of moving into white neighborhoods (p.21).

Quillian and Pager (2001) found whites and Latinos overestimate the crime rates in predominantly black neighborhoods. Thus, stereotyping African-American neighborhoods as crime ridden contributes to racial segregation (p. 749). Results from Quillian and Pager's (2001) study indicate that as the percentage of the population of young African-Americans increases, so does the perception that crime increases (p. 740). This stereotyping of black youth to criminal activity can be partially traced to images of African-Americans in local television news stories. Entman (1990) reported 76% of all local television stories about African-Americans were categorized as dealing with crime or politics. This depiction of African-Americans systematically fosters racism and general emotional hostility towards blacks (p. 332). Entman (1990) found in a single week of local news in Chicago, using all stories that depicted events caused by blacks or events that centrally involved African-Americans, 41% were categorized as crimes of violence committed by blacks. These stories stimulate fear of blacks, contributing to racial discrimination of Blacks to the present day (p. 335-336).

The media is not alone in perpetuating negative images of African-Americans. Political communications of all types repeat messages with racial overtones. The infamous 1988 television ad run in opposition to Democratic candidate Michael Dukakis criticizing him for allowing the furlough of prisoner Willie Horton while governor exemplifies this. A menacing picture of African-American Willie Horton was used to demonstrate this creating an image of the black criminal in whites' minds (Hurwitz & Peffley, 1997, p. 377). Hurwitz and Peffley (1997) contend the disproportionate accounts of African-Americans related to crime are more likely to contribute to reinforcement of negative stereotyping of black people (p. 394). These negative images of blacks as criminals contribute to whites' views on crime and racial beliefs. These "pictures in the head" of white respondents of blacks as violent people reinforces negative racial views (Hurwitz & Peffley, 1997, p. 395).

Feagin (1991) contends through his research that middle-class African-Americans still experience discrimination through avoidance actions, rejection actions, such as poor service, verbal attacks, physical threats, harassment, and attacks by white supremacists (p. 102). Feagin (1991) examined 37 in-depth interviews from a larger study of 135 middle-class black Americans in Boston, Buffalo, Baltimore, Washington D.C., Detroit, Houston, Dallas, Austin, San Antonio, Marshall, Las Vegas, and Los Angeles (p. 103). Results indicated all types of mistreatment were reported. Most common in public accommodations included rejection/poor service. Verbal or physical threat discrimination was most likely by white citizens or police officers (Feagin, 1991, p. 104). Feagin (1991) documents excessive surveillance was reported by African-Americans as they shopped. This excessive surveillance and lack of courtesy of clerks portrays the burden of being African-American in public places (p. 107).

African-Americans feel disenfranchised when it comes to the legal system and the enforcers of this system. Henderson, Cullen, Cao, Browning, and Kopache (1997) analyzed a telephone survey conducted in Cincinnati, Ohio in the fall of 1991. One hundred three African-Americans and 136 whites completed the interviews (p. 451). Henderson et al. (1997) found more than eight in ten African-Americans felt they were more likely to be stopped by the police, jailed, and given the death penalty. Over 95% of the African-Americans stated they would be stopped and questioned if they were in a white neighborhood by police (p. 454). Not surprising given these results, Henderson et al. (1997) found African-Americans embrace liberal criminal justice philosophies, which focus on rehabilitation in a perceived inequitable system (p. 456).

Stewart, Baumer, Brunson, and Simons (2009) analyzed data collected in 1997 from 867 black children ages 10-13 from Iowa and Georgia (p. 861). Results from these data indicated African-American adolescents reported police racial discrimination was associated with neighborhood racial composition, socioeconomic status, and violence rates. Stewart et al. (2009) observed significantly higher rates of reported perceived racial discrimination from the police in neighborhoods characterized by higher affluence, higher rates of violence, and neighborhood populations higher with white residents (p. 867). Stewart et al. (2009) found certain characteristics with those African-Americans who perceived police discrimination. Being male, having prior experiences with police discrimination, prior arrests, having school suspensions, having parents who were discriminated by the police, embracing street code values, and residing in an urban neighborhood were all significant predictors of racially biased policing (p. 874). Brunson (2007) contends people who live in disadvantaged neighborhoods have a considerable risk of experiencing contact from the police either directly or indirectly due to aggressive crime fighting strategies to which they are exposed (p. 75). Brunson (2007) contends African-Americans are more likely to acquire unfavorable vicarious information from friends, family, and neighbors related to the police, whereas whites are more apt to seek their information from media reports (p. 74).

Brunson (2007) argues that urban black men's perceptions of the police are formed from unfair and disrespectful treatment from the police, along with being targeted at a high rate by the police. Brunson (2007) also contends that prior research has shown that people's views of the police can be formed by what others have experienced as well (p. 76). Brunson (2007) examined 40 African-American young men's vicarious and direct experiences with the police and how those interactions impacted their perspective of the police (p. 71). Findings from this study concluded that even though participants did not report hearing about police involved incidents on a daily basis, incidents with the police did occur often enough to generate high levels of resentment and mistrust. This study also found that even if the secondhand accounts of events were not true, the perception of the events reinforced the beliefs that the police were using discriminatory policing techniques (Brunson, 2007, p. 92). Crutchfield, Skinner, Haggerty, McGlynn, and Catalano (2012) argue when it comes to interactions with the police, if people feel they are mistreated or perceive they are not treated fairly, their future behavior and interactions with the police may be negatively affected (p. 181).

Schuck, Rosenbaum, and Hawkins (2008) posit vicarious experience by people can be shaped through the exchange of observations and information about police interactions creating an overall perception of the police. Thus, attitudes of the police are not necessarily created out of direct experience of individuals, they are also developed through information obtainment and observation (p. 500). In a research study conducted in 2002 with 479 participants through a telephone survey in Chicago, Illinois, Schuck et al. (2008) found a significantly more likelihood of fear of police and unwarranted harassment towards African-Americans and Hispanics compared to whites (p. 511). Shuck et al. (2008) highlighted that people who have strong, negative feelings of the police may be more likely to perceive police interactions as negative. African-Americans hold the most negative attitudes towards the police, regardless of recent experiences (p. 514). Findings from this study highlight the important psychological link between feelings about the police and what is happening in people's neighborhoods (Schuck et al., 2008, p. 515).

Crutchfield et al. (2012) contend children from "problem families" get more police attention independent of behavior, whether it is warranted or not. Previous contacts with the police and teens who associate with other people involved in criminal activity are more likely to experience police contact regardless of the legality of their own activities (p. 185). Police concentrate enforcement actions in neighborhoods with higher crime rates. This increases the likelihood that children living in these areas will experience more police contact (Crutchfield et al., 2012, p. 186). Crutchfield et al. (2012) conducted a research project in Seattle, Washington with eighth-grade students during the 2001-2002 school year to analyze police contacts (p. 187). Crutchfield et al. (2012) found that teens who had school disciplinary contacts were significantly more likely to have police contacts. Teens who reported they knew adults who drank, got high, or committed crimes within the last 12 months significantly increased the likelihood of police contacts. Data also showed that more cohesive, safe, resourced neighborhoods significantly reduced the potential for police contacts for blacks but not for whites. Higher grades reduced police contact probabilities for whites, but not for blacks (p. 193). Family patterns increased police contacts. Children with parents who had a history of juvenile crime involvement increased the odds of police contact by one third (Crutchfield et al., 2012, p. 194). Data from this research study concluded that black juveniles reported more deviant adults in their networks. Associating with these adults puts a greater risk of police contact because the police may associate them with these adults and assume they are involved in criminal activity as well (Crutchfield et al., 2012, p. 195).

Buckler and Unnever (2008) analyzed data from a 2001 New York Youth Survey, which was conducted by the New York Times and the New York Police Department with 18 to 26-year-olds living in the city of New York. The survey had a total of 721 respondents (p. 273). Data from this survey indicated prior negative contact with the police significantly increased perceived injustice. Participants who experienced a prior negative interaction with the police were two and a half times more likely to perceive widespread and unjust racial profiling. Those who had prior negative contacts with the police perceived the police favor whites over African-Americans by nearly three times the amount. Those who had prior negative contacts with the police were also four times more likely to believe the police force is more likely to be used on African-Americans than on whites (Buckler & Unnever, 2008, p. 276).

Weitzer and Tuch (1999) theorize residents' views of the police are shaped by where they live. Black residents residing in middle-class, low-crime neighborhoods where policing is less intrusive and abusive have different views than those in inner-city neighborhoods (p. 495). Weitzer and Tuch (1999) used three data samples from recent surveys conducted by three different sources from 1993-1995. Data were collected through telephone surveys. Results indicated an overwhelming majority of African-Americans, 80%, viewed racism among the police as fairly to very common compared to 56.4% of whites (p. 499). Renauer and Covelli (2010) found through their research study of 741 randomly selected participants residing in Oregon that African-Americans are significantly more likely to perceive the police make stops based unfairly on race/ethnicity than whites (p. 502).

Carr, Napolitano, and Keating (2007) conducted a research project with 147 participants in the city of Philadelphia in three high-crime neighborhoods using qualitative interviews and self-report questionnaires. Data found in this research included a sentiment from participants of negative feelings towards the police. These negative feelings were based on lived experience through encounters with the police. Some encounters included instances of excessive force (p. 461). Given these findings, it can be surprising that when these participants were asked what should be done to reduce crime, most respondents suggested putting more cops on the street. Even those who were most involved in street crimes were advocates of an increased police presence (Carr et al., 2007, p. 462). Carr et al. (2007) concluded youth living in high-crime neighborhoods have negative encounters with the police and legal system, however, many youths who are negative of the police perceive them as having a vital role in crime-reduction, and the police should concentrate more on fairness and justice than outcomes (p. 469).

Anderson (1999) conducted a research study of life on the streets of Philadelphia, Pennsylvania about the code of the streets. Anderson (1999) documented how black people are generally disenfranchised and this operates in the back of their minds. Black people who walk into stores, especially jewelry stores, can see this phenomenon. Sales people pay closer attention to them until they have passed inspection, while black males almost always are subjected to extra scrutiny (p. 17). Anderson (1999) found corner men talking about their parents' tacit acceptance of their kid's drug dealing. These parents may worry about drive-by shootings or the occasional drug wars and the possibility of their child's arrest by the police. They often worry about the police. Not just in the potential for their child's arrest but because the family, in some cases, relies on the drug money (p. 29). Anderson (1999) paints a picture of the code of the streets as a place where there is a profound lack of faith in the police and the judicial system. The police are often seen as protectors of the white society and do not care to protect the inner-city residents. The code of the street begins when one's personal safety becomes their own responsibility and the police influence ends (p. 34).

Anderson (1999) states respect on the street is viewed as a form of social capital in a place where other forms of capital have been denied or unavailable. The criminal justice system is largely perceived as two separate entities, one for whites and one for blacks. This results in profound distrust in that institution (p. 66). Feeling they cannot rely on the police for protection, black residents take personal responsibility for their own security (Anderson, 1999, p. 109). In this culture, anything associated with the conventional white society is seen as square. Untied sneakers, pants worn below the waist, hats worn backwards, and hoodies have all become a style to go against the conventional. This style causes their community to receive a bad reputation from conventional cultures, particularly with black males (Anderson, 1999, p. 112).

Anderson (1999) details how black youth walking the street wearing the same clothes that are commonly associated with gang members and drug dealers are stopped by the police and asked where the drugs are, even if they are not associated with these groups. Thus, causing anger towards the police as harassing and profiling (p. 104). Weitzer and Tuch (2002) posit four in ten African-Americans claim they are stopped by the police because of their race. Almost three-quarters of young black males from 18 to 34-years-old claim to have been racially profiled at least once during their lifetime (p. 443). Higgins and Gabbidon (2009) contend profiling can come in two forms. Intuitional profiling occurs when an organization, such as the police, look for a certain personal profile of people. A second form of profiling occurs when individuals derive a specific profile developed from personal experience (p. 78).

The 1964 Civil Rights Act made it unlawful to segregate or discriminate against anyone based on race, color, religion, or national origin in public accommodation settings. However, even after five decades of implementation and despite popular beliefs of equal opportunity in the United States, there remain disparities in how people are treated based on race, color, religion, and national origin (Brewster & Rusche, 2012, p. 360-361). Brewster and Rushe (2012) conducted a research project into restaurant servers in 18 restaurants resulting in 200 completed self-administered questionnaires (p. 368). The majority of these participants were reported to be white (86.2%) (Brewster & Rusche, 2012, p. 369). Data from these self-report questionnaires reported on average participants believed white tables were easier to wait on than black tables. Black tables in every case were considered to be below average tippers, and 63% of the participants reported they over-heard coworkers and managers make racist comments on at least one occasion (Brewster & Rushe, 2012, p. 372). Brewster and Rushe (2012) reported the data showed nearly 57% of the participants self-reported treating customers differently based on their race occasionally. Nearly 53% reported observing coworkers treating black customers poorly (p. 377).

Cultural bias and institutional bias continue to account for the unfair treatment of blacks throughout the United States. Dovidio and Gaertner (2000) found bias against African-Americans in simulated hiring decisions occurred most often when a candidate's qualifications were ambiguous (p. 318). Cultural bias can occur in many places and institutions. Crosby and Moni (2006) found college academic advisors were more likely to not discourage black students from taking overly ambitious course schedules in fear of being labelled racist. This in turn leads to these students struggling or failing classes by becoming over-burdened (p. 664). Kim and Zabelina (2015) posit most standard tests, such as the SAT, are normed using scores from majority populations. This can have unfair consequences for various racial/ethnic minority groups without norming a test for these groups (p. 130). Zeisel (1981) discovered disproportionate death sentences in Florida for murder. Forty-seven percent of black defendants, compared to 24% of white defendants were sentenced to death when the victim was white. There was also no white person on death row for murdering a black person, however, there were blacks sentenced to death when the victim was black (p. 460).

Implicit bias refers to unconscienced attitudes, both negative and positive, towards other people, groups, or ideas (Greenwald & Banaji, 1995, p. 5). Human history has demonstrated an association with darkness negatively and lightness positively. These associations may account for African-Americans receiving negative attitudes with the motivations of maintaining racial hierarchies in the modern Western society (Alter, Stern, Granot, & Balcetis, 2016,

p. 1653-1654). Levy (2017) contends we seem to have little control over our implicit attitudes, nor over the way they influence our behaviors. Unprejudiced people sometimes have conflicting implicit attitudes, which may cause them to perform morally significant actions which they would have avoided had their explicit attitudes controlled their behavior (p. 4).

Greenwald, Banaji, and Nosek (2015) contend there is a cumulative impact when one is repeatedly encountered by the same person. By accumulating over repeated occurrences with the same person, small effects can produce substantial discriminatory impact. These repeated occurrences can take place in employment settings with response to multiple job applications or performance evaluations in the same job. In educational settings through test and homework evaluations with the same students or in a health-care setting with the repeated patient contacts occurring in the same hospital or clinic. These cumulative impacts may also occur out on the street with the police [or in the courtroom with prosecutors and judges] (p. 558). Banakou, Hanumanthu, and Slater (2016) found through their research that implicit bias can also be controlled. Through virtual body transference, Banakou et al. (2016) found white females who were given a dark-skinned virtual body diminished their implicit bias towards dark-skinned people for at least one week after the experiment (p. 10).

Hall, Hall, and Perry (2016) suggests the research on implicit bias shows the general public, above and beyond the police, favor whites over blacks, however, they may not be aware of this cognitively (p. 176). People may act out on stereotypes without conscious awareness or malicious intent. These stereotypes are not held by whites alone, however. Thus, combating racial prejudice in society as a whole may well need support by larger socialization efforts in our society (Hall et al., 2016, p. 178).

Gardiner (2000) interviewed African-American people who were outraged by the treatment they received while traveling through airports in America. Interviewing one individual, Gardiner (2000) learned of an African-American who was returning from Jamaica to the Newark airport when she was asked by customs to search her luggage. Other passengers were allowed to continue walking through customs without being searched, but she and her sister, along with seven of eight other black women, were stopped for search. This individual was then ordered into a private room where customs agents searched her body, probing intimate areas through her dress (p. 1). The logic behind the extensive search was explained to this black woman that customs inspectors assume African-American women are more likely to work as "mules" for drug smugglers (Gardiner, 2000, p. 2).

Gabbidon and Higgins (2007) contend consumer racial profiling takes two forms. When a racial or ethnic minority is provided poor service in retail establishments, or in the worst case of being denied service (p. 2). Gabbidon (2003) argues racial profiling in retail stores comes in the following forms: mistaken identity, extra scrutiny while shopping, additional identification requirements for check or credit purchases, unnecessary use of force, and blanket policies enacted to handle minorities (p. 361). Gabbidon (2003) states society reacts to people differently because of a labelling process. When it comes to racial profiling, the media and police have tagged African-Americans as criminals requiring additional scrutiny (p. 347). Dabney, Dugan, Topalli, and Hollinger (2006) posit the practice of profiling can be unconscious or unmotivated stereotyping (p. 647). People engage in social thought processes all the time to discern intent and behaviors of others. Profiling is a specific social cognition process directed at determining who has or is likely to commit a crime (Dabney et al., 2006, p. 652). Dabney et al. (2006) conducted an observational research study in a retail pharmacy/drug store located in Atlanta, Georgia (p. 654). Results indicated that despite intensive training and specific instructions to ignore shopper's demographic characteristics, observers were unable to resist implicit cultural stereotypes in shaping their selection of potential shoplifters. Observers disproportionately focused on non-white adolescent males (Dabney et al., 2006, p. 665-666).

The institution of education can also play a factor in the direction youth go. However, in this setting, many black kids who do well in school are negatively associated by their peers as acting white (Anderson, 1999, p. 93). Anderson (1999) interviewed kindergarten, first grade, second grade, and fourth grade teachers during this research. At about first grade, according to these teachers, some students become invested in the code of the street. Others who were well-disciplined maintained an interest in subject matter and took instructions from their teachers. However, by fourth grade, nearly three quarters of the students have adopted the oppositional culture or the code of the street (p. 317).

This dichotomy gets less clear when an African-American puts on the police uniform and swears to uphold the laws of the land. African-American police officers receive dual hostilities. One from the inner circle of white suspicion within the police agency and a more vicious one from some African-American citizens. Calls of being a "house nigger" to "you've sold out, you especially should understand." In response, one African-American officer replies, "No, I don't. My brother wouldn't do what you're doing" (MacDonald, 2003, p. 70). MacDonald (2003) interviewed African-American police officers and commanders from eight different police departments. What MacDonald (2003) found was a resounding rejection of anti-cop propaganda that is becoming a hindering problem on black progress (p. 84-85).

Policing in the United States

It can be argued that slave patrols were the first type of policing in the United States. Southern colonies developed systems of social control to maintain the institution of slavery by enforcing restrictive laws. The primary function of these early slave patrols was to apprehend runaway slaves and protection of the white population from crime committed by slaves or slave insurrections (Dempsey & Forst, 2008, p. 10). Early slave patrols were common by the early 18th century in the South. In 1704, South Carolina authorized the first slave patrol due to many white males being summoned into the militia to protect from a feared Spanish invasion. The slave patrols were groups of ten people who were exempt from militia duties (Turner, Giacopassi, & Vandiver, 2006, p. 185). These well-armed men and women patrolled by horseback and were tasked with inspecting each plantation within their district at least once a month and seize any contraband possessed by the slaves (Dempsey & Forst, 2008, p. 12). The first organized police force in the North was created in Boston, Massachusetts in 1838. Other police departments followed, including New York City in 1845 and Philadelphia in 1854 (Dempsey & Forst, 2008, p. 13). The Wichita Police Department was formed in 1871 (J. Espinoza, personal communication, August 29, 2016).

Police officers now come from many ethnic and racial backgrounds and various social upbringings. Like all human beings, they develop certain biases throughout their lifetime, from familial, community, society, as well as their jobs. Police officers are assigned daily areas to patrol. For that designated tour, they are responsible for anything that threatens or disturbs that area. Police intervention into others' lives becomes the central focus of their jobs. This authority over others is ultimately backed by force (Waddington, 1999, p. 297).

Negative encounters throughout their careers, including witnessing death and violence firsthand, can have long lasting effects on how they perform their jobs. Karlsson and Christianson (2003) conducted a phenomenological study into how police officers' traumatic experiences on the job affected them throughout their careers. Types of traumatic events included armed threats, traffic accidents, murders, suicides, and taking children into custody (p. 422). Long-lasting consequences associated with these traumatic events caused officers to feel depressed, guilty, withdrawn, and irritable (Karlsson & Christianson, 2003, p. 431). These added stresses can have a profound effect on how police officers react to future citizen encounters. Frustration with the criminal justice system and health care services can also have an effect on police officers. Mclean and Marshall (2010) conducted a study to see how officers dealt with mental health problems and services for citizens. Results indicated officers felt powerless with unsuccessful outcomes, complex responsibilities, and extended roles, which left them feeling as if they did not help anyone (p. 65). This only adds to the stress and frustration of police officers.

Bolton and Feagin (2004) argue police officers of today are encultured in a world that pits an "us" versus "them" view of the world. Officers isolate themselves from "civilians" while off-duty and create a tough-male crime fighter image with a strong loyalty to fellow officers. Due to the fact they often deal with street criminals who are disproportionately minorities, these negative encounters harden their stereotypical views instead of challenging them (p. 121). Officers have seen this play out over the last decade. When officers are assaulted and killed based on the uniform they wear, they feel isolated and on edge. An opposite effect of these interactions can occur from the perspective of the minorities experiencing the heavy police presence. African-American officers reflect in their neighborhoods that it seems like the police are always taking someone to jail. Officers do not come to do good things, which causes residents to learn to fear the police and be careful in their presence (Bolton & Feagin, 2004, p. 45).

Other studies have investigated the effects that police supervisors, top management, and citizen distrust have on altering the police culture (Ingram, Paoline, & Terrill, 2013, p. 383). Glomseth and Gottschalk (2009) point out that police officers learn their values spending long periods of time watching how other police officers do their job, eating with them, and socializing with them. There are dangers with young officers becoming influenced by old cynics who have negative and biased views of the administration and the public they serve (p. 6). Cancino and Enriquez (2004) conducted a research study with 18 patrol officers through in-depth interviews on peer retaliation among officers. Officers were interviewed on their perception of "street justice" and why they do not report abuses of other officers. Common themes were identified, such as the "the police code" of not "ratting out fellow officers," even if they feel those officers went too far. Others indicated the lack of trust for many people and only cops understand what they do (p. 327). Officers made statements, such as, "We're a brotherhood and we need to protect each other." Preserving solidarity among officers comes from officers refusing to report misbehavior and maintaining the code of silence. Street justice to some officers is normalized behavior and it becomes a morally and culturally accepted police practice (Cancino & Enriquez, 2004, p. 328).

Heck (1992) explains why police officers do not tend to report other officers' deviance. There is a functional solidarity and sense of oneness that is experienced by frontline officers. Officers perceive themselves as the minority, victimized by both the public and the administration. In response to these thoughts, police officers tend to tighten their closed fraternity and impose an artificial code of conduct to preserve harmony among their ranks (p. 255). If an officer does cross the line and reports misconduct, they are labelled a "snitch" by their peers. When rejection from peers occurs, the subculture seeks to punish the officer, deterring any potential risk of new snitches, and further solidify the solidarity of the group (Heck, 1992, p. 256). If a snitch is discovered, that individual becomes a non-functional member of the organization. These individuals become anomalies to the subculture, practically assuring their career will be short lived. To remain an officer without a support group would be an incredible feat of emotional stamina (Heck, 1992, p. 268).

Waddington (1999) postulates that police officers may say one thing in the privacy of the police station or in their squad cars, however, carry out things against those private thoughts in interactions with the public. However, if police perform their duties in racist fashion, it can be attributed to racist talk produced and sustained in the confines of these private spaces with other police officers (p. 288). Waddington (1999) argues the police routinely exercise coercive authority in ways that would otherwise be construed as illegal. Few people would feel entitled to approach people in public and demand for them to account for their time. Even when officers are providing service, they routinely violate the privacy of those they serve by demanding to know facts surrounding each incident (p. 299). According to Waddington (1999), police demean the suspect they chase similar to armies demeaning their enemies during war. Using terms, such as "scumbag" or "scrote," becomes a part of the culture when police officers come into conflict with marginal groups in society (p. 301).

MacDonald (2003) argues the police merely focus their enforcement objectives in the areas with the most criminal activity. MacDonald (2003) illustrates Harlem, New York as an example. When the citizens cried out for help from the police to do something about the continuous drug dealing destroying their neighborhoods, Mayor Giuliani and Chief Bratton developed new ways to combat problems using computer aided technology, Compstat, to pinpoint recurring crime spots. The police did not see the problem as "black" or "white," they only saw drug dealers. The perspective of the police was one of "good people" and "bad people" (p. 27). To illustrate how numbers can be skewed to make conclusions in any debate, MacDonald (2003) illustrates how claims of racial profiling along the New Jersey turnpike tell one version of the events. New Jersey State Troopers were doing heavy enforcement of speed violations and turning these stops into drug interdiction stops in one of the heaviest traveled South to North routes of drug smuggling veins leading to the Northern East coast cities. Critics called it racial profiling and the politicians shunned the practice. However, a separate research study designed by the Public Service Research Institute in Maryland and commissioned by the New Jersey attorney general determined through photo and radar of nearly 40,000 drivers found blacks made up 16% of the drivers on the turnpike and 25% of the speeders in the 65-mile per hour zone where the profiling complaints were most common. Blacks accounted for 23% of the stops along the turnpike by the troopers during this study. This study only counted speeders who were at least 15 miles over the speed limit. The results indicated African-Americans were not being stopped disproportionately (p. 31-32). MacDonald (2003) also found African-American state troopers stopped the same proportion of black drivers as their white counterpart troopers (p. 84).

MacDonald (2003) also found that 77% of New York blacks approval rating of the police occurred when heavy enforcement in troubled neighborhoods was occurring. These ratings were in direct contrast to the anti-police propaganda from activists and the press in a Justice Department study at the time (p. 47). MacDonald (2003) conducted in-depth interviews with black police officers and commanders from eight police departments across the country to gain an understanding from their perspective of policing (p. 84). One African-American detective from Brooklyn responded, "It's really hard now. Anyone can say, 'You fuckin' cops, you fuckin' cops, I pay your salary.' You have to be a doctor, a psychiatrist, a bad guy, a good guy in one minute. You have to understand the plight of the black man, the plight of women, the plight of gays, and not piss someone off and lose your job all in the course of a day." Another San Antonio hostage negotiator hears things like, "Aw, c'mon, bro', you tryin' to keep us down," he replies, "You have to make your own way. You make excuses, you'll never get anywhere," when he is working the streets (MacDonald, 2003, p. 87). The love/hate relationship of the police also changes with time. As a New York detective explains, "After 9/11, people would say, 'I love you'; they were naming their kids after you. It went from Motherfucker to Mister." When asked how this made him feel, he responded, "I was shocked. These people were bizarre, clapping every time they saw you. I went on a cruise and a woman asked to give me a hug." These types of gratitude can be short lived, however, at least in Flatbush where three months later it is back to "Motherfucker" (MacDonald, 2003, p. 88).

Without the support of top management for strong enforcement actions, some police officers will back off when facing racial tension. In Cincinnati and New Jersey in 2001, after a relentless race-based anti-cop campaign, stops and arrests plummeted. In New Jersey, consent searches for drugs and guns along the turnpike plunged. Without drug interdictions, the murder rate in Newark jumped 65%, and Cincinnati witnessed one of the bloodiest summers in its history (MacDonald, 2003, p. 91). The dichotomy between enforcement and perceived brutality can be explained by one officer's explanation, "You are trying to apprehend a bad guy and you break his arm. Now you're the bad guy? But if he gets your gun, he'll try to shoot someone, so is that excessive force? Say someone gets shot. Who do they go after: the perp or the cop? It won't be the perp because no one wants to deal with the bad guy. If you think about it every day, you go crazy, so you can't. You won't be in policing; you'll be out there scared to death, paranoid about everything" (MacDonald, 2003, p. 91).

Mastrofski, Reisig, and McCluskey (2002) point out that police work places officers in situations where they must tell people to do things they do not want to do. Incivility can occur in both directions and the police are not immune to human emotions. The police are also held to a higher standard when dealing with the public and expected to act professionally in verbal altercations (p. 519-520). Mastrofski et al. (2002) contend citizens who show disrespect toward officers, refuse to obey orders, or physically resist are at a greater likelihood of being disrespected by the police. Citizens who live in low-status neighborhoods, male of a racial minority, and younger in age are more likely to be disrespected by the police. Citizens who are in the company of those whom they have great familiarity with during a conflict are more likely to receive police respect (p. 526). Mastrofski et al. (2002) found through their research that white suspects were more likely to be disrespected by the police than minority suspects. Suspects have considerable influence on how they are treated from the police by their demeanor and actions (p. 539-540). MacDonald (2003) contends the police are the last people in our society that are willing to unapologetically and unambiguously make distinctions between the "bad" guy and "good" guys. From the police perspective, they are profiling "bad" guys based on repeated observations, however, to the public, this is seen as racially motivated profiling (p. 145).

Petrocelli, Piquero, and Smith (2002) used data collected by the Richmond, Virginia Police Department related to police stops and practices. This data contradicted conflict theorists' interpretation that police officers are more likely to profile poor, minority areas and conduct traffic stops. These data revealed officers were more likely to make traffic stops in high crime rate areas with crime rate being the more important factor (p. 8-9). Kochel, Wilson, and Mastrofski (2011) posit that it would be impossible to individually observe every interaction to determine the influence of the suspect's race on an officer's decision to arrest (p. 475). By merely demonstrating minorities are arrested more than whites does not establish the extent by which the suspect was arrested solely based on race. Other factors play into the decision to arrest, so confidence levels cannot hinge solely on suspect's race (Kochel et al., 2011, p. 476). Prior research has indicated fairly consistently specific variables increase likelihood of being arrested. These factors include: strength of evidence, severity of the crime, victim requesting an arrest be made, and suspect's demeanor (Kochel et al., 2011, p. 477). Kochel et al. (2011) conducted a meta-analysis study using 27 independent data sets of prior research studies related to citizen's race/ethnicity and the likelihood of arrest from 1966 to 2004 (p. 481). The findings from this research concluded that racial minority suspects have a higher probability of arrest than their white counterparts (Kochel et al., 2011, p. 498).

Lytle (2014) conducted a meta-analysis study on the effects of suspect characteristics to arrest. This study confirmed Kochel et al. (2011) study, which found blacks, Hispanics, and males were significantly more likely to be arrested. Blacks were 1.4 times more likely to be arrested, Hispanics were 1.25 times more likely, and males were found to be 1.6 times more likely than females to be arrested. Lytle (2014) postulates that the high number of Hispanic arrests in the Southwest may be due to the potential threat of this group to the established power group. A surprising result of this study was the fact blacks in the South were not significantly more likely to be arrested, even with their recent history of treatment (p. 595).

Regoeczi and Kent (2014) conducted a research study to determine how police discretion was utilized. Data were collected through observational ride-a-longs with officers and interviewing officers immediately after encounters with citizens. Research dating back to the 1930s has indicated factors involved in police decisions to arrest or issue citations revolve around citizen demeanor, citizen characteristics, and officer characteristics (p. 191). Results from Regoeczi and Kent's (2014) study indicated approximately 31% of white citizens stopped received citations compared to 53% of blacks (p. 197). When accounting for citizen demeanor, data results showed 67% were given warnings when they displayed positive demeanor, whereas 61% of citizens who displayed negative attitudes received a citation (Regoeczi & Kent, 2014, p. 199). Comparing the data between white and black drivers showed 74% of white drivers who were courteous received a warning compared to 55% of the black courteous drivers. Data also indicated officers initiated contact with citizens based on the actions of drivers and pedestrians (Regoeczi & Kent, 2014, p.200).

Police discretion represents the ability to allow officers to decide whether or not they issue citations, make arrests, and even use force. There are certain characteristics which affect discretion. Organizational characteristics influence officer behavior by creating regulations designed to guide police discretion. These expectations are expressed to officers through supervisors and administration policy. Administrative policies limit the amount of discretion officers are afforded by creating restrictions and boundaries to the enforcement of laws. The most significant court case associated with police using lethal force discretion came in the 1985 Supreme Court decision of *Tennessee v. Garner*. This ruling restricted the amount of lethal force an officer can use in cases where the officer believes the suspect is posing or has the likelihood of posing serious injury or a significant threat of death to the officer or other citizens (Nowacki, 2015, p. 644). Nowacki (2015) used data from the Supplementary Homicide Reports from 1980 to 1984, along with the 1970 and 1980 census to do a research study. Using only U. S. cities with populations greater than 100,000 as of 1980 (p. 652), Nowacki (2015) found that administrative policy and police department size directly influenced deadly force incidents for total homicides by the police (p. 659). Nowacki (2015) argues policies limit police discretion and may also affect police culture by changing the way officers patrol and make arrests (p. 660).

To put this into perspective, policing policies were minimal or non-existent in the 1960's and 1970's. However, from the 1980's to the present, policy manuals in police departments have become hundreds of pages thick. Police officers have to follow more policies than they possibly could remember. These policies do make officers think before acting at times, but they also confuse officers as to what conduct is acceptable. Policies are a police necessity, but as we have seen in many police related use of force incidents, officers do not always follow these policies. Either through human error, forgetfulness, or intentionally some officers violate policy, which creates questions from the media and the public. These questions can evolve into critiquing an officer's actions based on assumptions or opinions from people who were not present during the incident. Policies are also not universal with all police departments. They are worded differently and allow some officers to do things while others are forbidden. For example, the ability to pursue a fleeing vehicle. Some departments allow this in certain situations while others have a "no pursuit policy" or limit when it is allowed.

The nature of policing necessitates officers be afforded discretion. Well-developed police guidelines cannot anticipate the complexity of all situations officers encounter. The multifaceted and varied encounters officers respond to require officers to exercise substantial discretion during the course of their daily duties (Beckett, 2016, p. 78). Beckett (2016) attributes the rise in incarcerations of the last few decades to the lack of police discretion through policy efforts. The two main policy changes were the war on drugs and "broken windows" policies. The war on drugs caused officers to arrest and incarcerate more people than at any other time in U. S. history. State and local police departments placed a greater emphasis on drug enforcement, which was encouraged by national-level politicians which included financial assistance. "Broken windows policing" urged police departments to get their officers to aggressively enforce low-level crimes, such as panhandling or lying on the sidewalk, to reduce continued criminal activity (p. 80). These policy revisions essentially took police discretion out of officers' hands to avoid procedural violations.

Schulenberg (2015) conducted a research project into police discretion by observing police officers firsthand through 637 hours of ride-a-longs from November 2011 to June 2012 (p. 251). Schulenberg (2015) contends to understand police use of non-arrest discretion, factors of encounter, and citizen characteristics become important considerations. Offense seriousness and a prior record of violent offenses are consciously used when making a decision to arrest or not arrest during an encounter (p. 258). Schulenberg (2015) found the officers in this study were less likely to use discretion in encounters with male citizens, longer duration of the incidents, and if the officer was male. Officers were, however, 1.8 times more likely to use discretion in situations involving older citizens. Uncooperative and under the influence citizens were more likely to be arrested, and emotionally distressed suspects were 1.3 times more likely to receive discretion from the officers (p. 261). Surprising in this study, disrespect for the officer was not a significant predictor of an arrest. Schulenberg (2015) posits that officers are trained during field training to dismiss disrespect and not treat it as a behavior requiring a response. Citizens exhibiting uncooperative behaviors however were 41% more likely to land a criminal charge than those who were cooperative (p. 262).

Callanan and Rosenberger (2011) conducted a research study using 4,245 interviews that were conducted in a California statewide household sample between March and September 1999. Interviews were conducted using a computer-assisted telephone interviewing system. There were approximately 100 questions regarding media consumption, fear of crime, opinion of the police, and other crime-related questions (p. 175). Results indicated participants positively correlated believing the police were fair and negatively correlated excessive use of force was a problem in their neighborhood. Participants who were a crime victim or had an arrest of someone in their household were less likely to view the police as fair. Household arrest and fear of crime related positively to a belief that police use excessive force in their neighborhood (Callanan & Rosenberger, 2011, p. 179).

Dai and Johnson (2009) evaluated data taken from a 1997 and 1998 telephone survey of 1,150 participants in Cincinnati, Ohio (p. 600). Results indicated previous contact with the police only affected satisfaction if the contact was of a negative nature. Negative natured contacts reduced the level of citizen satisfaction of the police as a whole. Expectations of how the police in their official capacity treated citizens includes refraining from being angry, hostile, or rude, however, a warm and friendly demeanor was not expected of officers. Even one individual officer who acts out in these ways can have a negative effect on the entire police organization in citizen satisfaction (Dai & Johnson, 2009, p. 607). Dai and Johnson (2009) also found that over-all citizen satisfaction of the police can be changed by using policing strategies, which attack quality of life issues regardless of whether or not these strategies actually affect crime rates. By merely reducing citizen fear of crime, police departments can increase their image and gain a stronger satisfaction rating among their citizens (p. 608).

Using data collected in a survey distributed in a large western city, Wehrman and De Angelis (2011) investigated the willingness of citizens to participate in community policing initiatives (p. 54). Results indicated African-Americans were more willing than their white counterparts to work with police. These results indicated whites view the police as a social and political resource, and when changes are made, it is to amend strained relationships between the police and minority citizens. Minority groups, on the other hand, stand to benefit from changes in police operations and are more willing to help move the change. Data also suggests people who knew their neighborhood police officer were significantly more willing to express an interest to assist the police. Those with direct exposure to the officers were more willing to become a part of a community policing program (Wehrman & De Angelis, 2011, p. 62).

Birzer (2008) conducted a phenomenological study with 32 African-American participants over a three-month period to find what they felt were important qualities for the police to possess. All of the participants selected for this research had previous police contacts (p. 201). Interviews with participants were used to uncover which qualities of police officers African-Americans felt were most important through their experiences (Birzer, 2008, p. 202). Results indicated three important themes became important qualities, which these African-Americans felt were needed for police officers. The participants felt the police needed cultural diversity skills, they should be good communicators, and officers should have human skills, such as sympathy, empathy, being personable, and being cordial (Birzer, 2008, p. 204). Birzer (2008) ponders the troubling quandary of how to effectively address this relational issue between the police and African-Americans communities. Although the literature has shed light on the topic, it has never offered long-lasting policy recommendations (p. 207). To many African-Americans, urban white police officers have come to symbolize racial oppression (Birzer, 2008, p. 208). One participant in Birzer's (2008) study suggested African-Americans and police officers should participate in cultural diversity training together. This setting would allow participants to potentially dispel stereotypes and myths between the two groups (p. 209). Birzer (2008) concluded the police are required to participate in qualifications with their firearms, there should be an equal importance applied to human skills, such as diversity, sensitivity, and human relation skills (p. 209).

Scholars identify citizen's age, race, class, personal experience with officers, and the type of neighborhood which citizens reside as the primary factors that shape opinions of the police. A single high-profile incident can seriously damage the image of a police department and can shake the public's confidence in the police when the media covers the story (Weitzer, 2002, p. 397). Weitzer (2002) conducted research on the public's perception of the police in the cities of New York and Los Angeles using Los Angeles Times and New York Times polls after major incidents of apparent police misconduct. The most dramatic of these events was the Rodney King beating in 1991. African-Americans' approval of LAPD dropped a full 50% between a 1988 poll and a poll taken in 1991 a few weeks after this incident (p. 398). In New York City, the 1997 sodomy and beating case of Abner Louima, the 1999 shooting of Amandou Diallo 49 times by four officers as he reached for his wallet, and the 2000 killing of Patrick Dorismond during a scuffle with police caused approval ratings of the police to plummet. Respondents in a poll done in 1997 before the first incident showed only 14% of African-Americans felt the police were doing a poor job. In an April 2000 poll, that number reached 52% of African-Americans thinking the police were doing a poor job (Weitzer, 2002, p. 402). Weitzer (2002) postulates incidents like these are now part of the cultural repertoire which African-Americans conceive of the police. The result of this includes African-Americans becoming less cooperative with officers and making them more predisposed to assume police misconduct allegations, even when the officer acted appropriately (p. 406).

To be eligible to be a law enforcement officer in the state of Kansas, you must first be hired by a law enforcement agency and then attend the Kansas Law Enforcement Training Center for basic police skills. To be eligible to get hired by a law enforcement agency, one must meet the following basic requirements: 1) be a United States citizen, 2) have no felony convictions, and not have certain misdemeanor convictions such as domestic assault, 3) be a high school graduate or equivalent, 4) be of good moral character, 5) pass psychological testing, 6) be free of any physical or mental conditions which could adversely affect your ability to perform essential functions as a police officer, 7) and be at least 21-years-old. (kletc.org, n.d.). The city of Wichita, Kansas also requires: 1) an aptitude test, 2) a background check, 3) a physical agility test, 4) an oral board interview, 5) a polygraph examination, 6) a home interview, 7) and a command staff interview, prior to being hired (Wichita.gov, n.d.).

Police Use of Force

Police use of force is a contentious and debated topic within the United States because it involves the execution of an essential function of the state in enforcing the laws while also affecting the public's attitudes and behaviors towards the government generally and the police specifically (Friedrich, 1980, p. 82). Friedrich (1980) postulates there are numerous different theories in how the police approach explaining use of force. The three primary approaches were illustrated as: the individual approach, the situational approach, and the organizational approach (p. 83-84). Friedrich (1980) defines each approach in this way. The individual approach explains police use of force by the characteristics of the officer. The situational approach uses specific characteristics of the situation in which the police encounter citizens to account for use of force. The organizational approach posits use of force is a product of the organizational setting or some aspect of the setting which it occurs in (p. 84). To better understand this premise, one must consider what an officer thinks before a use of force encounter. Every situation with use of force is different. An officer does not think force will be used necessarily on routine calls for service. However, a simple shoplifting incident may turn into a deadly force encounter at any point in a flash. If the suspect is armed and decides to use his/her weapon on an unsuspecting officer, deadly consequences can occur. On the other hand, if an officer radios in that they are involved in a shooting, responding officers are mentally preparing themselves while responding to assist the officer for a potential use of force encounter. Some officers use more force than others. While two officers can have similar encounters, one may choose to use force at a different level than another officer. Both officers may be acting within policy, however, one officer may have felt the need to escalate the level of force based on unique circumstances. Was the suspect larger and stronger than the officer? Did the suspect have skills in fighting or martial arts? No two scenarios are the same when it comes to police use of force incidents, so they need to be analyzed individually.

Morrison (2006) stipulates officers need to depend on a combination of supplemental department-based training along with pre-service training at the police academy for managing dangerous encounters with substantial risks to the public and themselves (p. 226). Johnson (2007) states police officers need to make quick decisions about roles or motives of individuals based on little or no information when they are confronted with situations. They must quickly assess who the victim is and who the offender is when handling disputes and crimes (p. 277). Using video footage from the reality television show *Cops*, Johnson (2007) found there was little evidence to support the effectiveness of determining who were the criminals and who were the non-criminals based on non-verbal cues. When police officers have contact with citizens, it is unlikely they are familiar with the baseline non-verbal behaviors of the people they contact. Individual differences in how people display non-verbal behaviors may influence the officer's perception. It is difficult, if not impossible, for officers to accurately detect the non-verbal cues of people they have never met. African-Americans often display higher levels of non-verbal suspicious cues, even when they are not involved in a crime compared to Caucasians (p. 286). This can have a negative effect of how an officer handles an incident involving an African-American.

Using the 1966 observational study conducted by Reiss for the President's Commission on Law Enforcement and the Administration of Justice, Friedrich (1980) analyzed these data from three police agencies. These data were accrued through 36 observers of 600 police officers over seven weeks in 1966. The three cities included in this study were Chicago, Boston, and Washington D. C. (p. 85). Friedrich (1980) concluded through 1,600 incidents of police encounters with offenders' force was used in 5% of the incidents. Just over 3% of the force was considered "reasonable," and in just under 2%, the force was considered "excessive" (p. 87). Friedrich (1980) acknowledged the data may have issues due to the fact that how officers act in the presence of the observers may be different than how they act when they are not being observed. Friedrich (1980) also points out that the data showed African-American police officers did not appear to use force much differently than white officers in this study (p. 96). Friedrich postulated that police officers, like many of us, respond to the actions of the people they meet. However, being in a position of authority, officers need to learn this position comes with added responsibility requiring officers to respond to people more judiciously, which in turn could make use of force much less of a problem (p. 97).

Terrill and Paoline (2012) acknowledge police use of force is permitted by society in the course of their duties to uphold the laws. However, there are limitations to the extent of coercive power the police may use in maintaining order and enforcing laws. The two components that guide how and when the police are allowed to use force come from the police department policies and the U. S. Supreme Court decision of *Graham v. Connor*, 490 U.S. 386 (1989). Police administrators define the parameters of the application of force in a use-of-force policy. These force continuum policies attempt to clarify what is considered objectively reasonable force (p. 39). Terrill and Paoline (2012) conducted a research project using a survey that was sent to 1,083 police agencies inquiring what their use of force policies stated in regards to force continuums. Of those, 662 police agencies responded (p. 44). Data drawn from these surveys reported 80% of those respondents relied on some form of force continuum (Terrill & Paoline, 2012, p. 45). Terrill and Paoline (2012) noted of the 476 agencies which outline a force continuum, there were 123 different permutations resulting in a great variety in how police agencies detail their policies in relation to levels of force and placement of tactics (p. 47). Also noted in the data were the differences in how restrictive some agencies are when compared to others in terms of allowing officers to use severe force only on actively aggressive suspects while other agencies took a more liberal approach, leaving a large amount of discretion to the officer.

Alpert and Smith (1999) explain the use of force continuum as how officers should escalate and deescalate the amount of force used on a suspect based on the amount of resistance they are receiving from the suspect. As the threat level from the suspect diminishes, the amount of force should also diminish.

Use of force policies also usually allow for officers to skip steps within the force continuum if necessary. This can occur when a cooperative subject suddenly produces a weapon and threatens the officer. Alpert and Smith (1994) document an example of a police use of force continuum. It starts with no force, officers' presence in uniform, verbal communication, light subject control (escort holds, pressure point controls, and handcuffs), chemical agents, physical tactics and the use of weapons other than firearms and chemicals, to deadly force and firearms (p. 60). Missing from this continuum due to date of the research is where the taser falls into the use of force continuum. Terrill and Paoline (2012) found the taser was in different places of the continuum. There were 115 of the 476 agencies in their research who put the tasers in different areas of their force continuums, starting just after verbal commands up to deadly force (p. 51).

Another change has occurred with the documentation of use of force encounters. Alpert and Smith (1999) noted a variety of use of force reports exist and vary from organization to organization. These reports can vary from a detailed narrative of what occurred leading up to the decision to use force, the suspect's actions, and the officer's response, or they can be a brief description in an officer's report (p. 64). Alpert and Smith (1999) point out that use of force is a unique activity of the police, which requires specialized knowledge and skill beyond and above the experience of the typical juror. Use of force experts in turn play a vital part in educating juries and judges in the reasonableness and legality of police officer conduct (p. 75). Terrill (2003) contends training protocols for police officers in use of force generally call for officers to begin as low as possible on the continuum and apply coercive actions as the situation dictates (p. 60). The concept of the use of force continuum is for officers to move up and down the continuum as the situation dictates according to the level or severity of the suspect's resistance (Terrill, 2003, p. 69).

The United States Supreme Court decision in 1989 of *Graham v. Connor*, 490 U.S. 386 was a decision that changed police tactics and approaches to use of force. This case occurred on November 12th, 1984 when Graham was having a diabetic onset of an insulin reaction. Graham asked a friend to drive him to a grocery store to purchase some orange juice. When Graham saw the line at the checkout counter was too long, Graham left without purchasing the orange juice, deciding instead to go to a friend's house. Charlotte, North Carolina Police Officer Connor observed Graham's hast in and out the store, and feeling this was suspicious, followed the vehicle Graham got into. In a subsequent traffic stop of this vehicle, Graham got out of the vehicle, ran around it two times, and passed out briefly after sitting on the curb. In the ensuing confusion, other officers arrived on the scene in response to Officer Connor's request for backup. One officer approached Graham and handcuffed him behind his back, ignoring Graham's friend pleading to get him some sugar. Several officers then picked Graham up, thinking he was just drunk, and placed him face down on the hood of his friend's car. After the officers became more frustrated with the requests to verify Graham's diabetic condition, officers grabbed Graham and threw him head first into the police car. Officer Connor finally received information that Graham did not do anything wrong at the store, so Graham was driven home and released. Graham sued, alleging officers used excessive force causing a broken foot, cuts on his wrists, a bruised forehead, a shoulder injury, and a developed constant ringing in his ears, which was caused by the officers.

The United States Supreme Court postulated there are two primary Amendments which affected this case. The Fourth Amendment's prohibition against unreasonable seizures of the person and the Eighth Amendment's ban on cruel and unusual punishment. These are the two primary sources of protection against physically abusive government conduct of constitutional protection. The United States Supreme Court directed to the Court of Appeals their review of the District Court's ruling against Graham must be vacated, and the case must be remanded to the District Court for reconsideration under the proper Fourth Amendment standard (*Graham v. Connor*, 490 U.S. 386, 1989).

Another United States Supreme Court decision affecting police use of force occurred four years earlier in the case of *Tennessee v. Garner*, 471 U.S. 1 (1985). On October 3rd, 1974, Memphis officers were dispatched to a "prowler inside call." Upon arrival, officers were directed to the house this was occurring by a neighbor who stated someone was breaking-in next door. One officer went around to the back of the house where he heard a door slam and saw someone run across the backyard. The fleeing suspect, Edward Garner, stopped at a six-foot-high fence at the edge of the yard. The officer, with the aid of his flashlight, was able to see Garner's face and hands. He saw no weapon, and though not certain, was "reasonably sure" and "figured" Garner was unarmed. While Garner crouched at the base of the fence, the officer shouted, "Police, halt," and took a few steps towards Garner. Garner began to climb the fence. The officer convinced Garner would escape if he made it over the fence and elude capture shot him. The bullet hit Garner in the head, and he later died on the operating table.

The officer was acting under Tennessee statute and was within department policy. The Tennessee statute at the time stated, "If, after notice of the intention to arrest the defendant, he either flees or forcibly resists, the officer may use all the necessary means to effect the arrest" (Tenn. Code Ann. 40-7-108 (1982). The department policy was slightly more restrictive but still allowed the use of deadly force in the case of burglary. The District Court found the officer's actions and the Tennessee statute constitutional. The Court of Appeals, however, reversed and remanded. The Court of Appeals reasoned officers cannot resort to deadly force unless they have probable cause that the suspect has committed a felony and poses a threat to the officers or a danger to the community if they are not apprehended. The state of Tennessee appealed to the Supreme Court, and the Supreme Court affirmed the lower court's decision (*Tennessee v. Garner*, 471 U.S. 1, 1985).

The Supreme Court decision in *Tennessee v. Garner* has changed the way law enforcement apprehend fleeing felons across the country. Tennenbaum (1994) states because of the *Garner* decision, laws authorizing deadly force by the police to apprehend fleeing, unarmed, non-violent, felony suspects needed to be eliminated as they violated the Fourth Amendment (p. 241). Prior to *Garner*, police officers were allowed to use any means necessary to prevent a fleeing felon from eluding arrest. After *Garner*, police now must believe two conditions exist before they can shoot a fleeing felon. They must believe the crime involved the threatened use or use of deadly force or there is a substantial likelihood that if an apprehension is delayed, the suspect will cause death or serious bodily harm to another (Tennenbaum, 1994, p. 242-243). The effect on justifiable police homicide rates following the *Garner* decision were profound. Data from 1976 through 1988 in the Supplementary Homicide Reports showed a reduction in police homicides by more than 16% (Tennenbaum, 1994, p. 257).

Patrol officers rarely encounter violence from the public. They are, however, occasionally summoned to scenes where violence has occurred, and it is seldom directed towards them. There are few serious injuries sustained by the police or public in such encounters (Bayley & Garofalo, 1989, p. 6). Bayley and Garofalo (1989) conducted research in the summer of 1986 in New York City observing patrol work in three precincts (p. 3). Their research documented 120 potentially violent mobilizations where clear indications of violence existed. Of these encounters, 27% involved observations or reports of fighting in progress, 22% involved weapons, 3% included injuries while the remaining incidents involved a variety of things ranging from a rowdy crowd to mentally disturbed people (Bayley & Garofalo, 1989, p. 6). During these encounters, there were 11 cases of force used on the officers by assailants and 37 encounters where the police officers used force on citizens. The force used by the officers were almost exclusively acts of restraining or grabbing people. Firearms were not used during this research study (Bayley & Garofalo, 1989, p. 7). Bayley and Garofalo (1989) opine police are called to incidents where tempers are flaring and citizens in these conflicts are not always receptive to calm reasoning. Officers are wary the conflict can be redirected towards them, so they are trained to quickly assert their authority in such situations (p. 9).

MacDonald, Manz, Alpert, and Dunham (2003) suggest police officers, when arriving on a call, rarely know what they will encounter. Officers cannot make assumptions that those they encounter will either be cooperative or uncooperative when they arrive on the scene of an incident. The likelihood that officers may encounter violence or uncertainty is the reason officers are trained to maintain control of situations and quickly assess them. Police use numerous ways to control people, and the primary ability they have to set them apart from citizens is the authority to use physical force. There is a fine line between using necessary force and excessive force when police achieve legitimate objectives. Officers are required to make split-second decisions, which can be later viewed as unnecessary. Determining what level of force is necessary to make an arrest can be problematic. Although most citizens agree reasonable amounts of force can be necessary to ensure public safety, when an officer uses force which is considered excessive or unwarranted, the public approval for police authority comes into question (p. 119-120).

MacDonald et al. (2003) used all reported use of force reports in the Miami-Dade Police Department from 1996-1998 to determine which types of calls police used force most (p. 122). Results indicated officers used significantly higher levels of force on calls such as burglaries, larcenies, vandalism, and fraud offenses compared to domestic disturbances. MacDonald et al. (2003) surmised the reason for this was officers are more mentally prepared for a confrontation on domestic disturbance calls and are more easily able to take control of the situation. Moreover, when officers receive calls of violent crimes, they are more likely to arrive with more officers and a significant show of force. This increased presence can diminish any threat of suspect resistance. This allows officers to diffuse the incident with minimal force. In situations involving property crimes, officers may not be mentally prepared for physical violence to occur when things escalate (MacDonald et al., 2003, p. 126).

Terrill and Reiseg (2003) argue there is a consistent theme in the research on policing. Officers compartmentalize various geographic areas within which they behave according to their environment and not the suspect's characteristics. This may result in more force being used in high-crime and disadvantaged neighborhoods. Areas of high disadvantage are more likely to display behaviors of disrespect towards officers, causing higher levels of police use of force in these areas (p. 296-297). Terrill and Reiseg (2003) conducted research in 24 beats in the cities of Indianapolis and St. Petersburg using trained observers who were assigned to ride with patrol officers (p. 298). Over 3,330 police-suspect encounters were recorded during this study. For their purposes, police force was defined as acts that threaten or inflict physical harm on suspects (Terrill & Reiseg, 2003, p. 299). Terrill and Reiseg (2003) did not attempt to decipher whether any observed use of force incident could be judged excessive or not excessive (p. 301). Results from this study indicated officers were more likely to use higher levels of force when interacting with criminals in high-crime neighborhoods and areas of disadvantage independent of statistical controls or suspect behavior. The theory is problem areas correspond with dangerous places and dangerous places coincide with officer safety (Terrill & Reiseg, 2003, p. 307). A second theory is officers may be more likely to resort to force because, in these types of neighborhoods, it is the manner in which conflict is resolved. Officers may feel it is easier to get away with using force in distressed and high crime neighborhoods compared to other neighborhoods (Terrill & Reiseg, 2003, p. 308).

Jacobs and O'Brien (1998) posit there are two conflicting approaches to police violence. The conventional assumption is police violence is a reaction to encountered violence, so police killings are a necessary response to the hostility they must control. A political approach suggests police violence should be more prevalent in areas where racial or economic divisions with political consequences are severe. Diminished efforts to control the police occur when the privileged are threatened by the disorderly potential of the racial or underclass. Political explanations suggest stratified cities with larger percentages of minorities will have more police killings because dominant groups have more to lose from threats of public disorder coming from minority groups (p. 839). Jacobs and O'Brien (1998) contend 53% of the people killed by police are blacks, so if city mayors are black, police administrators will be more likely to curb police violence (p. 843). Analyzing FBI data for police use of deadly force resulting in death in the United States in 1980 with cities of populations over 100,000, Jacobs and O'Brien (1998) found murder rates, population, and divorce rates were consistent predictors of use of deadly force by the police. Other political variables that did not appear to influence the total rate of police killings include percentage of black residents and the presence of a black mayor (p. 851). Jacobs and O'Brien (1998) did find that having a black mayor did lower police killing of blacks (p. 858).

Nowacki (2015) postulates officers who have a great deal of discretion may allow bias to affect their decisions in use of force encounters. Such biases could convince an officer that some suspects are more dangerous than others, causing a preemptive use of force. Many of these biases supplement extralegal factors, such as race (p. 646). Given there are higher levels of crime in disadvantaged neighborhoods, police officers may perceive African-Americans as more dangerous than other races and maybe less resistant to use lethal force against them (Nowacki, 2015, p. 650). Nowacki (2015) found through his research that cities that have more restrictive policies tend to have fewer lethal force incidents against African-Americans, whereas department size was not statistically significant in lethal force being used against blacks (p. 657).

MacDonald (2003) interviewed numerous police officers to determine how race affects officers' decisions to use force. While officers need to acknowledge there are racists among them, a number of events are portrayed as racists actions based solely on the race of the officer and the race of the victim. As one New York officer replied to the killing of Amadou Diallo, "With a situation like Diallo, you have to make a split-second decision, and it can change your life. Sometimes officers make mistakes. But do you hold them liable as racist persons? That's where the stress comes from: you can't make mistakes" (p. 92). MacDonald (2003) postulates that police officers need to do a better job in teaching officers how to control their temper and emotions to cut down on excessive use of force situations. In the case of Abner Louima, had the officer not let the challenge to his authority affect him, the excessive force he delivered in the form of a toilet plunger would never have happened. The accusation that this incident was racially motivated is contradicted by the fact this officer was engaged to an African-American lady (p. 138).

Broome (2014) contends police officers involved in deadly force situations act under rapidly evolving and dynamic circumstances, which involve a variety of mental, physical, and emotional aspects (p. 158). Using a phenomenological method of research to better understand how this type of event unfolds for a police officer, Broome (2014) conducted research with three participants who were involved as police officers in deadly force situations while in the line of duty. This study required a verbal "re-living of the experience" from each participant, as the researcher surmised this approach would yield the greatest amount of data (p. 165). One participant officer explained the use of deadly force usually begins with an alert that the situation is becoming dangerous due to unfolding threatening conditions generated by a violent person (Broome,

2014, p. 167). Broome (2014) contends much of the officer's thinking is strategic and tactical. Officers take in as much information as possible to help them interpret and understand the unfolding incident as accurately as they can. The officer tries to strategize as much as they can as events unfold, to take positions and actions that would promote the surrender of the suspect while simultaneously reducing exposure to harm from the suspect. Officers view themselves in a dichotomy between the "good-guy and bad-guy" (p. 175).

Broome (2014) found all three of the officers had mixed conclusions about their experiences, and none of them thought the shooting was a good thing (p. 176). Frustration and anger in one officer occurred in reaction to how others viewed the shooting. It is plausible that this officer needs to accept the post hoc judgments by others who do not understand that shootings are very dynamic, complex, and frightening incidents, and those who have not experienced them firsthand will lack the perspective to adequately judge officers who have had this lived experience (Broome, 2014, p. 177). Broome (2014) opines that police officers who have experienced deadly force in the line of duty become different officers thereafter. Once an officer has killed another human being, the officer becomes one of a few who have done it. This can mean they "know" things that both citizens and other officers who have not been involved in deadly force will not quite fully comprehend. Even when an officer is exonerated, they feel they have gone through something unique, which they alone can fathom. Officers in this study felt only those who have experienced deadly force themselves would ever fully understand them (p. 178).

Jefferis, Butcher, and Hanley (2011) conducted a research study on perceptions of police use of force in an urban university located in the Midwest. A videotaped arrest of a young African-American male at a bus stop was made by a local Cincinnati news team in April 1995. This video was then shown to students in an introductory social science course, and participants were asked to complete a survey based on what they viewed. Participants were only told the event they would be watching was a real arrest (p. 84). Jefferis et al. (2011) found those participants who were more supportive of this aggressive police practice were less likely to view the actions of the police in this incident as excessive (p. 92). Jefferis et al. (2011) concluded that participants' perceptions of the police and their previous contacts with the police were directly related to their perceptions of this specific use of force incident. This study, however, did not measure attitudes of the police prior to viewing this video (p. 93).

Holmes (2000) argues when it comes to recognizing the distinction between reasonable and excessive force, few citizens have the knowledge to do so. Independent commissions and data collections procedures provided an array of descriptive evidence, however, they have not had rigorous methodological approaches done to allow for reliable conclusions about this issue (p. 348). Smith and Holmes (2003) recommend citizen review boards will increase accountability within police departments. By involving citizens in the investigation process, there is an increased likelihood of punishment for misbehavior on the part of the police and ultimately fewer instances of brutality (p. 1037-1038).

Schuck and Martin (2013) used data from the Chicago Alternative Policing Strategy, which randomly sampled 479 participants based on prior contact with the police, perceptions of the police, race, gender, and age. African-Americans and Hispanics were over-sampled to allow for accurate racial group comparisons (p. 223). Results indicated that although more whites were stopped by the police in this study, African-Americans and Hispanics were more likely to perceive injustice in those contacts. The results were similar when the participants had contact outside their neighborhoods. Here, again, African-Americans and Hispanics felt these contacts were perceived to be an injustice (p. 232).

Simulator Use

Broome (2011) contends if we really want to get the officer's perspective of what it is like to experience deadly force, there needs to be a methodology to analyze the subjective perspective (p. 140). Broome (2011) conducted a research project to evaluate the effects of "real life" deadly force encounters with police cadets to understand their lived-experience of the events (p. 144). In the category for time distortion, one participant responded, "Everything happened so quick, you don't get much time to think and make decisions." While another participant responded, "Everything kinda slowed down a little bit" (Broome, 2011, p. 147). Another participant could not remember how many shots they actually fired during a scenario (Broome, 2011, p. 148). Broome (2011) argues an emotional shock was experienced by all of the participants from being involved in the surprise attacks during these scenarios. These emotional shocks created perceptional distortions, changes to psychomotor performance, attention focus, vulnerability, and vigilance in varying degrees to the participants (p, 151). Broome (2011) noted that this experiment fell short of measuring the psychological impacts of real-life police shootings (p. 154). However, the use of simulated scenarios to better understand police use of force incidents and how citizens react to these encounters can only be safely analyzed in a research environment.

In a Department of Justice report, Reaves (2016) analyzed state and local law enforcement training academies and found 64% of them used a computerized firearms training system as part of the officer cadets' curriculum (p. 5). Reaves (2016) found 99% of U. S. police academies incorporated some form of reality-based use of force training. This type of training allows cadets to practice critical decision making, execute standard operating procedures, and under duress in real conditions employ potentially life-preserving tactics (p. 6). Furtado and Vasconcelos (2006) argue simulation attempts to represent one phenomenon by means of another. It can be a useful means to measure, demonstrate, evaluate, test, and predict with decreased cost and risk. Numerous organizations have used simulators for training personnel, such as the aeronautical and nuclear industries and the military. Simulators have been shown to be good teaching tools, especially for complex jobs with high risk and cost (p. 63). Furtado and Vasconcelos (2006) evaluated the use of simulators used by tactical managers for police force allocations according to the crime in each region. Experiments of this type could not be performed in the "real world" due to high risks, which could result in the loss of human lives. With this reality, simulators for teaching and decision support is a fundamental tool for law enforcement (p. 65).

White, Carson, and Wilbourn (1991) conducted research on the training effectiveness of M-16 military trainees through simulators. The purpose of this research was to determine if the use of simulators could teach marksmanship skills effectively, thus reducing costs and training time for recruits (p. 177). The Multipurpose Arcade Combat Simulator (MACS), which was developed by the Army Research Institute, is a system which uses a demilitarized M-16 rifle with a light pen, connected to a low-capability personal computer. Computer-simulated targets are displayed on the personal computer, and "hits" are registered from the light pen (White et al., 1991, p. 178). White et al. (1991) conducted research with the assistance of 247 participants who enrolled in the Air Force Security Specialist technical training course. The control group of 80 participants did their training in the traditional way on a live shooting range. The remaining 167 were trained through the MACS system (p. 179). Results indicated the MACS system of training was effective to bring participants with little or no weapons experience up to qualification standards for marksmanship. Those who used the MACS system showed scores equal to the control group making the system a practical instrument for saving time and money (White et al., 1991, p. 182).

After the February 1999 shooting of Amadou Diallo in a Bronx, New York neighborhood, many researchers started to investigate shoot/don't shoot decision-making. Correll, Park, Judd, and Wittenbrink (2002) used a video game which simulated situations where police officers are confronted with an ambiguous but hostile target, which puts the participant in a position to decide whether or not they should shoot. African-American or white subjects appear unexpectedly either armed or unarmed in a variety of contexts. Forty undergraduates from the University of Colorado at Boulder participated in this study. Ten African-American and 10 white models were used for targets. They appeared four times each in the game. Twice with a gun, either a silver revolver or black 9mm pistol, and twice with another object, such as a silver aluminum can, silver camera, black wallet, or black cell phone. The four targets were randomly superimposed with random objects. Background images were an intentional diverse assortment of photographs, such as a train station, park, hotel entrance, restaurant façade, or city street. Participants were to decide as quickly as possible whether the object the target was holding was a gun. If it was a gun, the participants were to push the right button labelled "shoot" on the box. If they determined it was not a gun being held by the suspect, they needed to push the left button labelled "don't shoot" as quickly as possible (p. 1315-1316). Results indicated participants fired on targets with armed African-Americans more quickly than white armed subjects. Participants also decided to not fire on subjects quicker when the target was white compared to if the target was African-American (Correll et al., 2002, p. 1325).

Plant and Peruche (2005) postulated stereotypes of African-American men to be violent criminals compared to white men may lead to racially biased interpretations of suspect behavior among police officers (p. 180). Plant and Peruche (2005) conducted a research study with 48 certified sworn police personnel in the state of Florida. Using nine black and nine white college-age photographs along with a picture of a gun or a neutral object, such as a wallet or cell phone, participants were to decide within the 630-ms time frame whether to shoot or don't shoot the subject based on a random photograph and random picture appearing on the computer screen by pressing a button (p. 181). Participant officers were initially more likely to shoot unarmed black suspects than white suspects. However, officers were able to eliminate this bias after extensive exposure to the program (Plant & Peruche, 2005, p. 182). Plant and Peruche (2005) postulate that the use of simulator training, such as the one they used, could help eliminate racial bias in the decision to shoot and improve over-all shooting accuracy in police officers (p. 183).

Plant, Peruche, and Butz (2005) conducted a study with non-black participants who were civilians and asked them to pretend they were a police officer. A video program was used, which showed half of the subjects as black and half as white, along with half containing a gun and half another object. Participants were to decide by pushing a button whether they should shoot or not at the subject (p. 143). Participants for this study were 125 non-black introductory psychology students. The program included nine black and nine white males, along with three pictures of guns and three pictures of neutral items, such as a wallet, cell phone, or camera (Plant et al., 2005, p. 144). Plant et al. (2005) documented the results from this study indicated participants made more errors with white faces than with black faces. Specifically, when a white face appeared with a gun, participants did not shoot. However, participants made more mistakes when the face was black with a neutral item than when it was white with a neutral item (p. 145).

Correll, Park, Judd, and Wittenbrink (2007) conducted a study where the participants were exposed to a news story about a series of armed robberies committed by either a pair of black men or a pair of white men to determine if reading an article affected bias in the decision to shoot. Seventy non-black participants from an introductory psychology class participated in this study (p. 1104). Like previous studies, the participants were instructed to push a button labelled "shoot" if the target was armed and "don't shoot" if the target was unarmed. Half of the targets were unarmed and half were armed. Half were also black suspects and half were white suspects (Correll et al., 2007, p. 1105). Results from this study indicated that by reinforcing racial stereotypes that link black people to danger and crime, it can have a dramatic effect of racial bias in the decision to shoot. Describing suspects as black rather than white in newspaper articles about violent criminals yields significantly greater bias in the decision to shoot (Correll et al., 2007, p. 1107).

Correll, Park, Judd, Wittenbrink, Sadler, and Keesee (2007) conducted a research study with 124 Denver police officers, 127 civilians, and 113 officers from around the United States using a video game simulator on shoot/don't shoot. There were 50 suspects photographed (25 black, 25 white) in five poses either holding a gun or holding another object, such as a wallet or cell phone (p. 1009). Results from his study showed officers exceeded civilians in numerous ways. Officers were quicker to make correct shoot/don't shoot decisions than civilians were. Officers were also better at differentiating armed suspects from unarmed suspects. Civilians also showed a tendency to favor shoot responses more than officers. Officers were equally likely to shoot or not shoot demonstrating less bias and a more stringent threshold when making the decision to shoot black suspects (Correll et al., 2007, p. 1015). Correll et al. (2007) did discover evidence through this study that although racial bias among the police is a concern, nothing from their data suggested that officers show greater bias than the people who live in the communities where they serve (p. 1015). One officer commented on the results of this study that the data makes sense since officers are trained to not shoot if they are uncertain and wait for greater clarity (Correll et al., 2007, p. 1020).

Through extensive training in many police departments, police officers understand threats and look at the suspect's hands to determine if they have a weapon or are reaching for a weapon. Police officers in many departments receive annual use of force and handgun training. Through these trainings, officers are trained to look for weapons. While there is a perception in the African-American community that officers will just shoot a black person, the reality is this does not occur at the rate it is believed. Officers can make mistakes and think they saw something they did not. These are human beings, just like the people they encounter. Human error is a part of living, however, United States police officers are some of the best trained law enforcement officers in the world.

The use of simulators to train law enforcement both in the police academy and in-service trainings has helped officers focus on the suspect's hands and identify weapons more accurately and quickly. Using role players in training sessions with paint ball-type weapons also allows officers to experience use of force on different levels. This is common training, which SWAT (Special Weapons and Tactics) teams use on a regular basis. Officers use their service weapons, which are modified to shoot rounds at role players that are tipped with a colored paint. Role players are given the same type of weapons for reality purposes. Officers experience situations as close to real as possible in a safe training environment to sharpen their skills. Training and technology has advanced over the last 20 years, giving police officers today the best preparation possible for encounters on the streets.

Correll, Urland, and Ito (2006) conducted a study to examine the manner in which stereotypes influence behavior by using event-related brain potential (ERP), which are fluctuations in the electrical activities in the brain that take place in response to specific stimuli (p. 121). Results from this shoot/don't shoot study replicated previous findings that participants were more likely to shoot armed blacks quicker than armed whites. Participants were also quicker to not shoot unarmed whites quicker than unarmed blacks. Participants who reported a stronger association with blacks and violence displayed higher biased behavior (Correll et al., 2007, p. 126). Correll et al. (2007) articulate there is a complex psychological process people go through when deciding when to shoot. Both threat perception and conflict detection play important roles, and more crucially racial cues promote bias shooting behavior because black targets seem more threatening and white targets conflict more strongly with the tendency to shoot (p. 127).

Peruche and Plant (2006) conducted a research study to examine police officer's explicit attitudes and beliefs about African-American suspects and their implicit responses. Peruche and Plant (2006) postulated that officers who have positive experiences with African-Americans in their personal lives or on the job may help eliminate racial biases and counterbalance negative stereotypes about African-Americans (p. 194). As a white police officer with many years of experience this has an interesting point. Having African-American mentors, African-American colleagues, dear friends, and an African-American niece, nephews, and Godchild, I do look at people more in a human way than criminal way. Officers who only associate themselves with same race/ethnicity friends outside of work settings may not understand other cultures. They may get confused about behaviors they are not familiar with. For example, African-Americans can tend to talk loudly. One African-American participant in this study,

AA-017, made this comment during the interview, "For one, I don't think they understand our culture. I think, you know, African-American people are a loud culture anyway." This can confuse officers of other ethnicities to believe a fight is about to begin, when in fact, it is a simple conversation between two or more people. Officers with a more diverse understanding can recognize each situation better and avoid a heightened sense that trouble is brewing.

Peruche and Plant (2006) conducted their research with 50 certified police officers in the state of Florida. The participants were to decide to shoot a suspect who appeared on a computer screen based on the presence of a gun or a neutral item appearing on the screen. To accomplish these decisions, participants were instructed to hit the "shoot" key if a gun was present or a "don't shot" key if it was a neutral object. Participants also completed a questionnaire about their on the job experiences and perceptions of criminality and violent behavior of black versus white suspects (p. 195). Extensive exposure to the simulations reversed early mistakes from the officers who were more likely to shoot unarmed black subjects compared to unarmed white subjects eliminating racial bias (Peruche & Plant, 2006, p. 196). Peruche and Plant (2006) posit officers' years of service and training on the job were related to less racial bias in the early trials of the shooting simulation. Officers were also likely to have fewer negative stereotypes of African-Americans if they had positive contact with African-Americans in their personal lives compared to those who only had contact during working times (p. 198).

In a more recent study, James, Vila, and Daratha (2013) found contradicting results. James et al. (2013) argued previous studies have several weaknesses when it comes to simulator studies. The first limitation was the test simulation lacked external validity. The second limitation was there is a difference between firing a gun and pushing a button. Firing a gun requires many more motor skills than pressing a button. Furthermore, there is no differences between pressing one of two buttons. Participants in this study were placed in situations that closely resembled real-life deadly force encounters. Real Glock handguns, which were modified for use in a simulator setting were used (James et al., 2013, p. 196). Participants for three studies included 102 participants. Those who had at least five years of police experience or completed one tour of duty in combat infantry roles were considered experts. Participants with no police or military time were considered novices (James et al., 2013, p. 197). Participants were given holsters and belts and taught how to operate the weapons system prior to beginning the study. Participants were also instructed on the rules of engagement of a police officer in deadly force (James et al., 2013, p. 200).

James et al. (2013) found the results from these three experiments produced contradictory results to previous studies. In these experiments, participants took longer to shoot black suspects than white suspects (p. 202). James et al. (2013) found results from these three experiments revealed racial and ethnic bias in the opposite direction than would be expected. Across all three groups of participants, military, civilian, and police officers were significantly slower to shoot black suspects. In two of the experiments, participants were significantly more likely to shoot unarmed white suspects compared to black suspects. In one experiment, participants were also significantly more likely to fail to shoot armed black suspects compared to armed white suspects (p. 204). James et al. (2013) also found police and military participants showed better accuracy and were more interactive during the scenarios shouting commands, such as "drop your gun." Noted also was the superior command presences these participants showed compared to the civilian participants (p. 205).

Ma, Correll, Wittenbrink, Bar-Anan, Sriram, and Nosek (2013) conducted research to determine how the effects of fatigue correlated to decisions to shoot in a simulator setting. Using a typical night of sleep reported by the participants and the amount of sleep the night before the experiment as a basis for the evaluation (p. 519). Ma et al. (2013) discovered officer cadets who reported less sleep the night before the experiment showed greater negative racial bias in terms of reaction time, errors, and sensitivity during the experiment (p. 522). Ma et al. (2013) suggested that police officers were still able to override racial stereotypes of blacks with danger and respond to the objects the suspect was holding when making a decision to shoot (p. 523).

Realistic interactive simulator training can be used to elicit understanding and emotions. Shapiro and Gianakos (2010) found the use of movies activated emotions in physician participants. Movie clips allow learners to reflect on their own attitudes and responses, which can reconnect learners to their original idealistic aspirations and motivations (p. 23). Shapiro and Gianakos (2010) argues emotions are the universal language which can help people bridge cultural differences and achieve mutual understanding and interpretations (p. 24). For these reasons, the use of simulator experiments with participants can create understanding of the others' lived experiences.

Hubal, Fishbein, Sheppard, Paschall, Eldreth, and Hyde (2008) argue role play exercises that are used to gauge social competency skills may be difficult to implement in many settings. This limitation shows the need for novel measures that can be administered with relative ease and simulate real interactions with other people to evaluate social competency (p. 1105). An exhaustive search of the literature did not produce any studies where a simulator was used to understand empathy or emotions through marginalization.

Cultural Empathy and Qualitative Research

Chen (2013) contends "acquiring another person's perspective" is an essential part of defining empathy. The first step to become more empathic towards other cultures is to understand who we are culturally. Then we can move to the second step of realizing the differences between other cultures and our own culture (p. 2267). Goleman (1998) describes empathy as emotional awareness. Emotions shape our perceptions and what we believe and do. These feelings affect those we deal with in life (p. 55). Empathy can be viewed as an interpersonal phenomenon. To accomplish this, we must: empathize with the others' situation and emotions, the other person experiences more than one's own emotion, the empathizer has the ability to see a similarity between what the other person is experiencing and relate it to a previous experience they have encountered, and have concern for the others' well-being (Chen, 2013, p. 2268). Chen (2013) argues empathy is the starting point in effective interpersonal communication. Empathy requires us to see what others' emotional states are and how others' perceive the situation involved. However, if we do not know anything about the others' culture, it becomes highly probable that we will make inaccurate predictions and interpretations of their behavior (p. 2269). In essence, we must see things from another's point of view to develop empathy (Chen, 2013, p. 2270).

Segal (2007) argues when people have social empathy, they will promote social justice through the formation of practices, services, programs, and policies (p. 76). Segal (2007) posits there are three levels which build upon each other when developing social empathy. The building blocks begin with exposure to becoming aware there are differences between and among people. The strongest way to expose people is to have people interact with people who are different than them, which introduces people to others' lives (p. 77). The second stage occurs when people delve further into differences to better understand why they are different and the historical reasons for the differences. This stage is called the explanation stage. The third stage is called the experience stage. In this level, people gain a deeper understanding by actually participating in others' day-to-day lives to develop a fuller picture of what it is like to live as the other person (Segal, 2007, p. 78). Segal (2007) contends when we experience other people's lives, we are better able to see the complexities of other people's circumstances, and we become less likely to make harsh judgments about the choices some people have made (p. 78). Empathy is not about feeling good or bad for people, it involves seeing what a situation feels like based on analysis and explanation about a situation (Segal, 2007, p. 79).

Chen (2013) contends for us to better know and adjust to others we need to develop empathy. This can be done through role-taking of the other person. However, there are numerous things that can counter us from understanding the thoughts, feelings, and motivations of others, regardless of their culture. The most common trait of blocking empathy from occurring is constant self-focus. If we are consumed with ourselves, it becomes difficult to gather and reflect information about other people. Empathy is also a reciprocal phenomenon, which cannot take place if one of the people becomes defensive over the other's lack of interest (p. 2271). Cassels, Chan, Chung, and Birch (2010) posit social and emotional well-being requires the ability to feel empathy. The ability to react properly in social situations requires people to perceive what others are feeling and appropriately share those emotions (p. 309).

Cassels et al. (2010) state there are two types of empathy: cognitive and affective. Cognitive empathy focuses exclusively on recognizing and identifying another's feelings and ignores emotional reactions to the feelings of others. Affective empathy involves experiencing emotions that are similar to the other person, which can sometimes manifest in different emotions (p. 310). Soto and Levenson (2009) add the term emotional empathy, which is similar to affective empathy. Emotional empathy suggests the way to come to know someone else is through feelings, which can be done by experiencing a version of the emotion ourselves (p. 875). Empathy can develop in early childhood and continue developing through life in some. Others may be altered through peer relations and an increase to the broader cultural community, which affects their ability to show empathy and alter the way they respond to others in distress (Cassels et al., 2010, p. 312). Soto and Levenson (2009) concluded through their study that recognizing emotions of both in-group and out-group members when making dynamic, real-time judgments of others' emotions can be done equally. This finding suggests we can increase cooperation and communication in our growing multiethnic environment (p. 882).

Kasl and Yorks (2016) contend there are three educational tenets associated with empathy: learner's lived experience creates significant learning environments, empathy creates multiple ways of knowing, facilitating learning, and significant learning occurs through dialogue. Empathy becomes our pathway into different worlds (p. 4). In a learning environment, empathy can be obtained through sharing another's experience. Since it is not possible to accomplish the ideal mode of transmission by being another person to truly understand their lived experiences, the best mode of access into another's experience is through an experiential one. The other's felt world can be experienced through intuition and imagination (Kasl & Yorks, 2016, p. 6). It may not be easy to cultivate empathic space with individuals from other cultures due to perceptions that the other is deficient, unworthy, and outside the normal bounds. Accepting the other's perspective as credible becomes challenging in developing empathy (Kasl & Yorks, 2016, p. 8). Kasl and Yorks (2016) conducted a research project with 19 doctoral cohort students during their second year of study on other-knowing. The group was divided into groups, which exclusively separated whites from blacks in teams to study cross-racial empathy. Each team was to study race from a personal perspective in teams and individually. Teams then did presentations for the other team to better understand racial empathy (p. 9). In one scenario put on by the African-American team to help the white team understand, the white team acted out a scenario where the people with blue eyes were arrested and manhandled by the police in front of the black team. Following the exercise, white team members described loss of control and fear during the scenario. Black team members reported they could see this fear in the white people. Through this experience, white people grew more able to understand how racial others feel and developed an empathic connection (Kasl & Yorks, 2016, p. 10). Through this dramatization, one African-American student described how her beliefs were wrong about whites. She found whites' behavior was not intentionally hurtful or purposeful, whites were genuinely unaware of black experiences (Kasl & Yorks, 2016, p. 12).

Klimmt, Hefner, and Vorderer (2009) posit that non-interactive entertainment, such as films, novels, and video games, enable and invite people to become an integral part of the mediated world (p. 353). Playing video games, for example, stimulates the feeling of being a media character. One assumes the role of a soldier or police officer for example. People develop a relationship with the character they have assumed and no longer perceive the interaction as a game but rather experience the character and themselves as one in the same (Klimmt et al., 2009, p. 354). Klimmt et al. (2009) contend when people assume the identity of media characters, they develop a self-concept through adoption of perceived characteristics. For example, if the user identifies as James Bond, for that moment, they are James Bond. This means they attribute all of James Bond's physical attractiveness, strength, courage, and charisma to themselves (p. 356). Klimmt et al. (2009) concluded that through self-identification of characters, gaming experiences could induce players to change their self-concept towards the properties of those characters. Players' self-perceptions therefore can be altered, so they assume a different perspective in contrast to themselves (p. 358). Video games can represent a "true" occurrence of identification of others (Klimmt et al., 2009, p. 363). This form of experience can in turn allow players to assume the role of others to better identify with their lived experience and alter their understanding of each other.

Menzel, Wilson, and Doolen (2014) postulate to deepen student empathy, students can be immersed in experiential learning modalities about poor people and poverty (p. 1). Merrian, Caffarella, and Baumgartner (2007) state experiences including vicarious experiences and simulated experiences can create learning. Activities, such as simulations, games, and role-playing, can lead learners to a critical reflection of assumptions. Through critical reflections, people can examine the underlying beliefs and assumptions that affect how they make sense out of the experience (p. 144-145). Vandsburger, Duncan-Daston, Akerson, and Dillon (2010) attempted to capture this transformational learning process by having participants "walk in the shoes" of poor people. The study was designed through the use of simulation to help participants understand what life might be like for people living in poverty. The study simulated people who were unemployed, elderly, or disabled. Another simulation had the "bread-winner" of a family desert the family, which caused the poverty (p. 305).

Vandsburger et al. (2010) solicited 134 health and human services students as participants for the study. The simulation was designed in four 15-minute weeks where participants had to do various tasks, such as apply for welfare assistance, meet with a representative of an employment office and apply for work, or negotiate the payment of utilities within a certain amount of time (p. 306). Results from this study indicated participants were more empathic in understanding poverty's effect on the poor (Vandsburger et al., 2010, p. 312). Vandsburger et al. (2010) described the data results showed participants from the poverty simulation experience changed how the students felt about the struggles of living in poverty. They related to the daily experiences and hassles of the poor when they try to feed, clothe, and provide shelter for their families (p. 311).

Patterson and Hulton (2011) conducted a research study with 43 senior undergraduate nursing students using a simulation experience called, "Life in the State of Poverty" (p. 144). Participants assumed the roles of families facing poverty. This simulation was developed to sensitize participants to the realities of poverty stricken people. The task for the participants was to provide basic necessities and shelter for their families through four 15-minute weeks. These challenges included being recently unemployed, relying on welfare assistance, using food stamps, and possibly being unemployed and having to raise grandchildren (Patterson & Hulton, 2011, p. 145). Using qualitative methods through reflection of the experience, Patterson and Hulton (2011) found evidence that the nursing student participants changed their attitudes on the stigma of poverty, welfare, and disapproval for those who live in poverty. The participants also found they needed to become more involved in their communities with vulnerable people (p. 148). Patterson and Hulton

(2011) argue the use of well-planned simulation experiences can change participants' attitudes and beliefs and recommended the simulation as a good learning tool (p. 149).

Nickols and Nielsen (2011) wanted to investigate whether social empathy could be cultivated through poverty simulation (p. 24). This simulation experience was similar to the others where participants were given four 15-minute segments to provide food, shelter, utilities, and other expenses, as well as maintaining and caring for children (Nickols & Nielsen, 2011, p. 28). Nickols and Nielsen (2011) used both quantitative and qualitative analysis and found nearly all participants reported the experience as transformative. Participants developed more empathy for people living in poverty after the experience (p. 37). Nickols and Nielsen (2011) also found participants more strongly disagreed that poor people are lazy or fake illness to avoid working. There was significant change in the group's mean score when it came to greater empathy from these participants (p. 38).

Bachen, Hernandez-Ramos, and Raphael (2012) conducted a research study with students in three California high schools. Students used a game simulator named REAL LIVES, which allows participants to develop empathy and interest in learning about other countries by having them live simulated lives in other countries (p. 2). Bachen et al. (2012) postulated when a participant takes the perspective of another, they begin to identify with the character represented helping to develop empathy (p. 4). Bachen et al. (2012) argue other research studies have shown evidence that empathy can be learned, and identification can create good conditions for increased learning (p. 5). REAL LIVES simulation allows participants to live vicariously like a person from another country. This experience includes education, marriage, having children, confronting diseases and natural disasters, which people may encounter in those countries (Bachen et al., 2012, p. 6). Bachen et al. (2012) found from the results of this study that participants increased their sense of global empathy through identification with culturally and geographically distal characters (p. 16). Affective learning outcomes, such as empathy, can be promoted through the use of role-playing games more effectively than other types of learning strategies (Bachen et al., 2012, p. 17).

Blake (1994) argues students have not been exposed to the histories of various groups in the United States and their economic and social development. Students are uninformed about the realities of group status and the relationship to individual functioning, particularly when it comes to oppression, power, and the functioning social welfare system (p. 130). Blake (1994) contends students need to understand we all have commonalities and differences, and those differences need to be more thoughtfully and respectfully put into perspective. Gaining factual information about others broadens the students to move beyond themselves and improves factually based self-awareness (p. 133). The use of simulator experiences may help expose participants in this way and create empathy in understanding the others' lived experience.

Qualitative Research

Yin (2011) suggests there are five features of qualitative research that should be used to determine if this is the right approach to a study. All five can be applied to this study:

- Studying the meaning of people's lived experience.
- Taking the views and perspectives of people and representing them in the study.
- Documenting understanding of the conditions within people live.
- Using the existing or emerging concepts, which can explain human social behavior to contribute insight to the knowledge.
- Rather than relying on one source of knowledge, using multiple sources of evidence to better understand the topic (p. 7-8).

Creswell (2013) adds there are four basic sources of qualitative data collection: interviews, documents, audio-visual materials, and observations (p. 52). Each of these were documented in this study. Moustakas, 1994 (as cited in Creswell, 2013), opines phenomenological research occurs when the researcher collects data from people who have experienced a phenomenon, and they explain "what" and "how" the experience affected them (p. 76). Experiencing a phenomenon with a group of individuals who have all experienced the phenomenon is essentially what phenomenological studies consist of (Creswell, 2013, p. 78). Hennink, Hutter, and Bailey (2011) contend the primary focus of qualitative research is to understand experiences through the meanings that people attach to them and explain peoples' views and behavior associated to the topic (p. 10). This study attempted to accomplish both.

Methodology/Research Project Description

This research study was comprised with two groups of 22 and 20 partici-pants. Pre and post-interviews were conducted around a simulated interven-tion with all 42 participants in two forms. Twenty-two African-American participants experienced six use of force simulated scenarios, while 20 white police officers experienced six simulated scenarios exposing them to living as a second-class citizen. The design validity for this study was validated through evaluation of the themes through coding important commonality from the interviews produced by the participant's interview transcripts. All interviews were audio-recorded with permission and later transcribed. Par-ticipants were asked to read the transcripts and point out any possible mis-takes in their transcribed data. Creswell (2013) suggests using this method of triangulation by locating evidence in different data sources to document codes and themes. This form of corroboration allows the data to stand on its own and produce valid results. Creswell (2013) also posits researchers need to clarify their possible biases by commenting on past experiences, prej-udices, and orientations, which could shape or effect the interpretation and approach to the research (p. 251). The researcher acknowledged an extensive law enforcement background but pledged to allow all participants to inter-pret the experience in their own words.

Fraenkel et al. (2012) define the dependent variable as outcomes or results of the study (p. 265). These results are determined by assessing whether there were any effects to the group receiving treatment and whether that treatment made a difference or change (Fraenkel et al., 2012, p. 266). The independent variable for this research study were the 42 participants who went through the six simulation scenarios. Post-interview questions were focused on whether each participant's view of the other's culture was altered creating understanding and empathy, which was not present in the pre-interview stage.

This research project was primarily focused on how two distinct cultures understood the lived experiences of the other culture and was grounded in phenomenological research that describes common meanings among several people who experience a phenomenon (Creswell, 2013, p. 76). Understanding the factors that create embedded fear of the police within a large portion of the African-American culture when it comes to trust, arrest, imprisonment, and use of force is paramount to creating better understandings between these two cultures. With the assistance of the Wichita Police Department and Wichita African-American citizens, this qualitative research project sought answers to allow both cultures to better understand deeply embedded perceptions of how each culture feels. According to the 2010 United States census data, the city of Wichita has a black or African-American population of 11.5%, which amounts to approximately 42,000 people (United States Census Bureau, 2010).

This research study recruited 20 white police officer volunteers working within the city of Wichita to participate in pre and post-interviews related to their cultural awareness of lived experiences of African-Americans in the United States. With the assistance of an instrument (Laser Shot), interactive video scenarios were created that were meant to demonstrate incidences of being ignored, mistreated, and unwelcomed in everyday activities. Analysis of these police officers' experiences were done through post-interviews and transcript analysis. Data gathered through the interviews sought codes and themes, which the participants articulate through words on how the experience did or did not change their perceptions of how marginalized people live in the United States on a daily basis.

In the last few years, an unprecedented amount of media coverage within the United States involves police use of force, which resulted in armed and unarmed African-Americans being mistreated, injured, and/or killed, has created further divide between these two cultures. This study recruited 22 volunteer African-Americans living in the city of Wichita, Kansas with no prior police or military training through community group solicitation to participate in pre and post-interviews related to police use of force. With the assistance of an instrument (Laser Shot), these participants experienced police use of force video scenarios in an interactive format. A Glock handgun, mace, and taser equipped with a laser were used to determine when force was applied by the participants. The intent of the simulation was to expose African-American citizens to police officer field situations. Observations of these interactions were documented, and post-interviews were conducted to determine if any changes in use of force perceptions occurred through the participants' words. Data analysis was conducted through transcript review of common themes, which emerge from pre and post-interviews.

Support for the Research Approach

A phenomenological research approach was appropriate for this study. According to Creswell (2013) phenomenological studies explore with a group of individuals an experience which they all have experienced. Participants are empowered to share their stories and experiences, so their voices can be heard with minimal intrusion from the researcher (p. 78). Pre-interviews explored how African-Americans understood police use of force, and post-interviews determined if through a simulated experience of use of force scenarios their views have changed. In the same fashion, police officers participated in pre-interviews to understand how they felt about social issues, such as living in poverty or being marginalized in everyday encounters. Post-interviews determined if their views had changed through the simulated scenario experience.

Researcher's Perspective

As a white male police officer with 27 years of experience in various working capacities, I have experienced many incidents of use of force. When use of force encounters occur, there is likely little time to prepare. Your training and experience takes over, and you react as you have been trained to do. Americans have watched and witnessed the tension between many African-Americans and the police due to use of force incidents. Some of these incidents have resulted in the police officers not being charged with a crime, which has been followed by anger, protests, and riots. Numerous police officers have recently been ambushed and killed in retaliation for these incidents around the United States. While politicians and civil leaders have spoken out on this issue, little attention has been focused on how to create understanding and empathy between these two cultures.

As a researcher, my intention was to be aware of, monitor, and account for biases and pre-conceived notions during the interviews and simulations to let the participants explore their experiences in their own words. I pushed myself to say as little as possible during the interviews and let the research be primarily about the participants themselves, other than inquiring further with follow-up questions. This research was conducted a great distance from the researcher's residence to avoid bias in the research setting and allow the research to be conducted in a large metropolitan area. Avoiding other biases was done by inter-coder reliability. Kurasaki (2000) contends gathering a measurement of agreement through multiple coders related to how they apply codes to the text can be used as a proxy for validating the constructs (p. 179). This process can reduce researcher bias. For this research study, two colleagues from the Saint Mary's EDD program assisted in the inter-coder reliability phase. Diana-Christine Theodorescu ABD and Regina Brown ABD agreed to become inter-coders for this qualitative research project.

Researcher's Role

The researcher's role in a qualitative study is the prime research instrument, which requires awareness of potential biases and idiosyncrasies. These conditions can arise from the researcher's personal background, motives for doing the research, and personal filters, which could influence understanding of events and actions (Yin, 2011, p. 123). The researcher collects the data while the participants experience the issue under investigation. Detailed note taking and journaling becomes essential in documenting the events and interactions with participants. Researchers generally assume human beings interpret and perceive similar experiences in some form of commonality. Researchers seek to identify, describe, and understand these commonalities (Fraenkel et al., 2012, p. 432). Fraenkel et al. (2012) stipulate researchers doing phenomenological research need to get participants to relive their experiences in their mind and describe them during the interview session. These interviews should be recorded to allow the researcher to search through the transcripts from each participant to locate relevant and meaningful statements in the data (p. 433).

My role as the researcher in this study was to review pertinent literature on the topic of study to develop a stronger understanding of this dichotomy. As the human instrument collecting the data, I needed to create simulated scenarios, which were realistic and interactive to humanize the experience. I was responsible to ethically create scenarios with human participants in mind to avoid any harm coming to them. During the research process, my intention was to avoid as much personal bias as possible and report accurate results based on the participants' statements.

Project Design

This research project attempted to determine if empathy and understanding of two distinctly different cultures can occur with an interventional simulated experience. Scenarios using Laser Shot Inc. software and hardware were developed and chosen by the researcher and used in the research site of Wichita, Kansas. The researcher conducted pre and post-interviews with 22 African-American citizens and 20 white police officers to determine their understanding of each other's culture. Interviews were semi-structured to allow the participants to properly articulate their experience and feelings about the scenarios and to allow the researcher to probe deeper into the participants' feelings and to clarify answers. Data were recorded, transcribed, and coded to find the common themes of how the participants felt about the experience and any changes in their perceptions.

Population and Sample

Population

The city of Wichita, Kansas site was determined to be the best fit based on open access to police participants through the chief of police. Police culture in large police departments is different from small police departments and larger populations of African-Americans reside in large city settings. A large city was needed to properly address this dichotomy where recent events across the United States have occurred. Wichita is the largest city in Kansas and has the largest African-American population in Kansas. According to the United States Census Bureau, the city of Wichita has 382,368 people of which 11.5% are black or African-American (United States Census Bureau, 2010). Wichita, Kansas does not have the highest percentage of African-Americans as other comparable cities have, however, Wichita does have a large population of African-Americans who have experienced living in a large city as an African-American.

One population for this study included all African-Americans living or currently residing in the city of Wichita, Kansas. The other population was all white police officers working for the Wichita Police Department. The Wichita Police Department currently has 804 police officers, of which 707 are white (J. Espinoza, personal communication, August 31, 2016). The Wichita Police Department is led by a newly appointed progressive chief of police. Chief Gordon Ramsay wanted to be in the forefront on this current dynamic effecting people around the United States. Naming Wichita Police Department as an active participant in the research was approved by Chief Ramsay as long as the officers remain anonymous and their participation is voluntary (G. Ramsay, personal communication, September 30, 2016).

The city of Wichita was in a bad situation before the arrival of the new chief of police. There was little communication between the old chief and the community regarding relations. Chief Ramsay has started to change those relationships (L. Williams, personal communication, October 4, 2016). Instead of passively watching a Black Lives Matter protest occur in Wichita on July 17th, 2016, Chief Ramsay reached out to activist A.J. Bohannon and requested a barbeque of burgers served by the Wichita police officers. Chief Ramsay's plan was to create dialogue and not further division (Itkowitz, 2016, p. 1). This was the first time in recent Wichita history that a protest turned into a festivity. In further speaking with Chief Ramsay, he was unaware of any good or bad incidents of specific cultural relationship incidents in the city of Wichita (G. Ramsay, personal communication, September 30, 2016).

Sample

The purposeful sample drawn from these populations included 20 white police officers, along with 22 African-Americans who had no police or military training and were at least 18 years of age. Creswell (2013) describes a purposeful sample as one where the researcher decides who to select as participants and the size of the sample to be studied (p. 155).

Sampling method

Civil, community, and church leaders were sought out with the assistance of the Wichita Police Department to solicit volunteer participants for this research. A detailed description was circulated through the African-American communities to locate interested participants. Participants were informed in this document that their participation was voluntary and their names would remain anonymous in the reported data. Contact with community leaders was made to create collaborative relationships and explain the research project. The researcher requested these leaders notify colleagues and their group members of the upcoming project. Volunteers were sought once the proposal was approved, and the researcher reached out for volunteers requesting a variety of ages and backgrounds to volunteer. This study was not conducted in a college setting to avoid a small demographic of participants. The researcher accepted the first 22 volunteers who could make arrangements to attend during the assigned time frames. No preference was given to a specific individual or community leader, and no-one was excluded from participating.

An email was sent to all of the Wichita Police Officers soliciting their participation. Roll call announcements were added to each shift briefing encouraging the voluntary and anonymous participation with the permission of the chief of police. There was no preference given to specific officers who met the research criterion. Officers were chosen by the first 20 volunteers who were available during the given timeframe dictated by the researcher. Officers from four different bureaus with different levels of experience had the opportunity to participate. The hope was to have officers with a wide range of police and life experience volunteer for this study. Hennink et al. (2011) posit researchers should inform participants they have the right to refuse to take part in the study and will remain anonymous, the participants' data will remain confidential with the researcher, selection of participants should be done in a just manner, the research should contribute to the benefit of the participants, and the researchers need to assure the participants safety during the study (p. 77-78).

Power

Creswell (2013) posits qualitative sample sizes can vary between one and as high the researcher can accommodate depending on the study (p. 157). A sample size of 20 participants for this type of research study for each group is considered a powerful sample size.

Project Assessment

Theory of Effectiveness

The theory of effectiveness for this research study was through simulated scenario experiences of another culture's lived experience, cultural empathy and understanding can be created to help solve the current dichotomy between the police and African-American communities. New training methods can be developed to re-create this research to allow police departments around the country a new alternative to cultural training for police officers while simultaneously creating better understanding for African-Americans in how police use of force works. This could create better dialogue between these two cultures in tense times.

Hunt and Swiggum (2007) argued their research illustrates cultural competence cannot all occur in the classroom (p. 173). Gaining cultural empathy for others occurs in many different environments. This study attempted to vicariously experience the thoughts, feelings, and experiences of participants from another culture to determine if empathy can be achieved through simulated reproductions of another person's lived experience. The pre and post-questions were centered on whether a person can obtain empathy based on simulated experiences of another's life. Sarkis (2012) states more compassionate operations research is needed for topics that call for inquiry include risk, security, and resiliency management of communities (p. 361). The questions used in this study attempted to gain new knowledge and understanding between two conflicting cultures within society to mitigate their risks and security.

Procedures

The procedures for gathering data via interviews, which Creswell (2013) proposed were the following: (1) determine which questions would best answer the problem, (2) identify participants through purposeful sampling who can best answer these questions, (3) decide which method of interviewing is most practical to obtain the best data, (4) use adequate recording equipment and procedures, (5) use pilot testing to refine interview questions, (6) determine the best location to conduct the interviews, (7) obtain written consent from the participants, and (8) use good interview techniques (be respectful, courteous, a good listener, stick to the questions) (p. 163-166). Interviews and the simulation exercises were conducted at the Wichita Police Department in private rooms to avoid distraction and interruptions with the police officer participants. A local community building and church were sought to insure convenience for the African-American participants along with the comfort of not being in a police station and rapport building. Open-ended, semi-structured interviews with all participants occurred just prior to the start of the simulated experience and just after finishing the experience to assure the experience perceptions were "fresh" in their minds. Brunson (2007) contends in-depth interview techniques offer a unique opportunity to examine the meanings for those who experience events and to gain insight into the context and circumstances of the event (p. 76).

This research study began in the spring of 2017 with several trips to Wichita, Kansas by the primary researcher. Due to unforeseen circumstances, the researcher had to produce the video scenarios with the assistance of volunteer role players to assure the scenarios were recorded correctly. The researcher spent another week in Wichita, Kansas, meeting with stakeholders and developing relationships with community leaders and police personnel to set-up for the study. Research was conducted for each group of participants during the course of consecutive days. One group of participants was completed before the other group began in this study to avoid unreasonable delays, which could have allowed participants time to talk to each other about the simulation experience.

Instruments

Fraenkel et al. (2012) contend interviewing is a form of instrumentation, which allots the advantage of being able to clarify any questions and allows the participants to expand on answers that are particularly important or revealing (p. 120). This study included multiple semi-structured interviews with the participants to capture the affective nuances of experiences that cannot be garnered through quantitative means.

The Laser Shot scenario-based police shoot/don't shoot training projector was utilized as an instrument for the African-American participants to gain a better understanding of how complicated use of force for police officers can be. The scenarios were designed around officer involved incidents, which make them as real as possible in a simulated event. All scenarios are currently used in the law enforcement field to teach police officers how to better interpret threats and react accordingly to resolve the situation according to state laws, the constitution, and policy and procedures. The use of video recording was also an instrument of this study. Participants were video recorded during their scenarios in the Laser Shot portion of this study with written consent. If consent was refused, recording did not occur. Scenarios based on feeling marginalized was the instrument used for the police officer participants to gain a better understanding of how African-Americans experience life as a marginalized citizen. These scenarios were based on six common themes in the literature which African-Americans have experienced marginalization. Through an exhaustive literature review on how African-Americans have experienced living in the United States, these scenarios were developed to best elicit marginalization to white police officers.

These simulated scenarios were equivalent in the sense both sets represented the others' lived experience in everyday human interactions within their culture. Both sets of scenarios showed different types of interactions, however, both sets represented each culture's lived experience. While an expert panel review may have provided new and different scenarios to demonstrate marginalization and use of force, practicality on making different scenarios and prior data would not necessarily confirm these options based on what the literature had documented.

These scenarios were designed to determine if the dependent variable of experiencing another's culture had an effect in participant's understanding of how that culture lives every day. Understanding how different cultures live can create cultural empathy, which can allow people to better communicate through dialogue to resolve conflicts. Cultural understanding allows people to judge a particular situation or different way of living, while cultural empathy creates shared feelings and emotions of cultural differences. It cannot be assumed one or all six would create a change to the independent variable, thus a variety of scenarios were needed to determine the effects of the experience. However, living as another person through simulation may allow people to open their minds to alternative emotions. The use of simulated equipment has not been attempted in past research to measure changed perceptions in this manner. Through personal observation of both police officers and citizens, I have seen the effects of how people interact with use of force scenarios through verbalization and actions to resolve conflicts. Attempting to create a simulated marginalization scenario was new to the literature, so results have not been documented. The literature did not provide a road map to understanding marginalization or cultural understanding. Through personal observation and prior experience, I believe this research breaks new ground into better understanding this dichotomy in a new way. This format was designed to be a safe environment where physical altercations would not occur. Participants had the opportunity to assume the role of the other without leaving the confines of a safe location.

Description of Scenarios

There were 12 scenarios developed for the purposes of this study. There were six scenarios for the African-American participants and six for the police officer participants. The following police participant scenarios are outlined here:

- The participant was walking through a county fair and noticed large amounts of security officers following him/her as they casually move through the fair.
- The participants received poor service at a restaurant they have taken a friend to catch up on lost time. This included slow or no wait staff assistance and rude or condescending looks by the staff and management.
- The participant went to a jewelry store to look at diamonds and was treated poorly. There was a male manager requested to assist, added security in close proximity, and questioning about the participant's ability to pay for the jewelry.
- The participant was walking down a street and witnessed people move to the other side of the street when he/she approaches in an attempt to avoid them. Notice people roll up their car window as they approach and generally avoid eye contact or communication with the participant.
- The participant was in an airport setting returning from a trip and encountered a border patrol agent and was pulled aside from her/his group and questioned extensively about being a drug smuggler based on profiling.
- The participant was on a family vacation in a non-English speaking country when a family member of theirs had an unknown illness and needed treatment in the emergency room. Staff in the emergency room was difficult to communicate with, generally rude, and unsympathetic, and they never received treatment while others with lesser injuries/ailments were treated.

The following are the African-American scenario outlines:

- The police were called to a home after her husband comes home drunk and threatens her life.
- A man was locked out of his house because of an argument with his girlfriend. He began banging on the door. The girl called the cops to remove him.

- The police were alerted to a mentally unhinged woman who trespassed onto private property.
- An officer went to handcuff a criminal and requested that you watch her back.
- A patrol car was riding by a complex when they noticed an argument between two motorists.
- An irritated driver became angry when she was pulled over for speeding in a neighborhood and asked for identification.

Participants were warned that some of these scenarios may contain profanity or graphic depictions. If they felt they are unable or unwilling to hear or see such things, they were released from the experience and the research prior to beginning the study.

Justification

All of the police scenarios were developed by Laser Shot Inc. for police training depicting "real" police incidents and interactions with the public during their daily patrol. Some have been personally experienced by the researcher and the researcher's work partners. For these reasons, the scenarios depicted realistic events, which all of the participants experienced to a gain better understanding of the others' lived experience. Using simulation to explore gained empathy, however, was not supported within the scholarly research data.

Validity

Fraenkel et al. (2012) define validity in qualitative research as the appropriateness, meaningfulness, and usefulness of the inferences based on the data researchers collect (p. 458). Validity for this study was conducted through the use of the triangulation technique. Codes and themes were developed through the dissection of the interview transcriptions, notes taken, and observations made. This method allows for verification of the facts and descriptions being presented in the research data. Validity was determined through analysis of the literature review findings with the results from the data collected in this study. A third method of validity was conducted by asking the participants to review the transcripts of the interviews to verify the proper data was present in the manor they presented it.

Reliability

Fraenkel et al. (2012) contend reliability is based on the consistency of infer- ences over time, location, and circumstances (p. 458). Reliability for this study was done through the use of computer assisted qualitative analysis (CAQDAS) software to develop codes in the transcripts which can show patterns of con- sistent answers. Reliability was also established by allowing participants to re- view the transcripts from the interviews to assure accuracy. Transcription of the audio recordings was also reviewed by the researcher to gain reliability in the data. Once all of the data were compiled, statements were disassembled into codes using the assistance of CAQDAS software and reassembled accord- ing to common patterns and themes in the data. Using these themes, a narra- tive was developed by interpreting the data according to headings found through the analysis of the data themes. The narrative presented the findings of the study as the data dictated. Once the narrative was complete, conclusions were made based on the analysis of the data.

Coding and Analysis

Description

Hennink et al. (2011) identify two purposes for coding the data. First, it allows the researcher to locate the range of issues raised in the data and to make sense of the meanings attached to these issues brought by the participants. Second, codes allow researchers to locate every place in the data where a specific issue is discussed by topical marking to index the entire data set (p. 217). Creswell (2013) suggests codes can represent information the researcher expected to find before the research began, information that surprises the researcher and was not expected, or conceptually interesting or unusual data (p. 186). Fraenkel et al. (2012) suggest the researcher formulate themes with the data by grouping codes as they develop either during or after the coding process (p. 480). Cres- well (2013) adds a popular approach to analysis of themes is done by identify- ing five to seven general themes from the codes. Several codes can be aggregated to form a common idea creating a theme (p. 186).

Data collected for this research was done through semi-structured interviews with participants. Fraenkel et al. (2012) define semi-structured interviews as a structured interview combined with open-ended questions (p. G-8). These interviews were audio-recorded and transcribed by a professional transcriptionist. The data were then disassembled through CAQDAS software and codes and themes of the data were organized in cluster meaning units to identify and categorize the themes. Themes and codes of empathy and understanding of another's lived experiences were analyzed to determine if cultural understanding can be accomplished through simulated experiences. Two inter-coder reliability evaluators were sought to confirm the codes and themes the researcher had identified and possibly identify missed themes in the data. Both of these inter-coder reliability colleagues are current Saint Mary's University doctoral candidates whom have been taught qualitative coding through their course work at Saint Mary's University. Both inter-coder reliability evaluators have non-law enforcement backgrounds and both are female. One inter-coder reliability reader is African-American and the other is white.

Justification

The coding and analysis procedures that were used in this study are consistent with those recommended for use in qualitative research by Creswell (2013), Fraenkel et al. (2012), and Hennink et al. (2011).

Design Validity

This study was designed to explore the experiences of a select group of police officers and African-Americans citizens before and after simulated scenarios depicting the others' lived experience. In-depth interviews with participants enabled the researcher to explore the essence of their experience and how it altered their perceptions through their words and meanings. Following the themes during the interview process and probing the participants to clarify as best they can the true meanings of their answers was necessary to avoid confusion of meanings later during the analysis portion of the study.

Data analysis procedures included transcription of the recorded interviews by a professional transcriptionist, note-taking, participant review of their transcripts, member checking, and two outside reader reviews. These procedures were suggested by Creswell (2013) to strengthen validity and reliability (p. 251-252). Additional threats to validity may have included difficulty in accessing participants due to weather or mechanical issues, technological problems, scheduling conflicts, time constraints, unexpected events affecting participants, and unexpected life events affecting the researcher.

Ethical Issues

Fraenkel et al. (2012) remind researchers of some important ethical considerations when conducting qualitative research. Researchers must keep the identity of the participants protected. Participants should be allowed to withdraw from the study if confidentiality cannot be maintained. Care should be taken to prevent data from embarrassing or harming participants, and participants should always be treated with respect (p. 438). Protecting human participants is of primary concern in research. Approval for this research to be conducted came from the St. Mary's Research Review Board prior to beginning. Obtaining voluntary informed consent from all of the participants through a written document was used to allow the participants to understand the purpose and nature of this research. Assessing any possible psychological risks associated with the scenario based use of the Laser Shot experience was addressed prior to implementation. Participants were warned in writing and through verbal communication that some of the scenarios use profanity and depict graphic images. If they were offended easily, they were allowed to withdraw from the study. Participants were selected on a voluntary basis from specific groups which were needed for this research. Participants were given the opportunity to refuse to be a part of the research and allowed to withdraw at any point. Confidentiality of the participants' identity was done by assigning a code to all documents, including audio and video recordings associated with this research. All data collected were secured by the researcher to keep participant confidentiality, and participants were requested to review the data collected on them prior to documentation of the data in the research results. There was not any deception or concealment utilized in this study. This study was not intended to produce undesirable consequences, however, there was the possibility that participants may have felt offended.

Maintaining individual interviews with participants allowed private conversations versus a group interview. Some participants may not have felt comfortable speaking their feelings or beliefs in front of others. Being able to maintain anonymous private space for individuals to speak freely without the added pressure of others observing or challenging their thoughts remained the best way to gather the necessary data for this research study. All participants were granted pre and post-interviews around the simulated experience of the other's culture.

While it would take follow-up interviews months or years down the road to determine if the effects of this intervention were sustained by the participants, it is not feasible for the researcher to do. There remain issues of distance, participant belief changes from incidents or encounters with the other culture that could alter belief systems, and mortality. It is hoped this research study provides valuable data that allows future researchers to build upon and strengthen.

Results

The findings section is the culmination of 22 African-American participants' semi-structured pre and post-interviews of police use of force simulated experiences, along with 20 white police officers from the Wichita Police Department who experienced simulated scenarios of marginalization treatment. These next chapters summarize interview samples, along with code numbers for each participant. Demographical data are added to better understand the sex, age, and experience of the participants. The other chapters are specific to the research questions, the results that emerged from the data collection, coding, and thematic analysis processes. Each theme is summarized in detail and supported by specific quotes which are meant to convey the experiences.

The purpose of this research study was to see if simulated scenarios of experiencing what it is like to traverse through another's culture can create cultural empathy and understanding. Of specific interest was whether greater understanding could be gained through experiencing another's phenomenon through their own account of the experience. The research question for this study is: Do simulated experiences change cultural empathy allowing police officers to better understand what being marginalized feels like and African-Americans to better understand how use of force works in police events? The short answer to this question is yes. Chen (2013) contends we must see things from another's point of view to develop empathy (p. 2270). As these chapters will lay out, there were dramatic changes with both groups of participants in their thoughts and understandings of each other after experiencing these simulated videos of living as the other. The majority of the participants had a change in their original understanding following the simulated experience.

Sample Profile

There are two samples for this study. The first were 22 African-American participants who did not have any police or military experience, and the second were 20 white police officers from the Wichita Police Department. Requests were sent out through community members and the police administration for 20-25 volunteers meeting the specified criteria. No participants were denied access to the study, and all 42 were the first to agree to participate. The African-American participants were assigned codes AA-001 through AA-022. The Wichita police officers were assigned PO-001 through PO-020.

There were 12 female participants and ten male participants for the African-American sample. The age range ran from 18 to 83 years of age with an average age of 54.6 years old. The educational levels ranged from a high school degree to three participants with Masters Degrees. There were four female participants and 16 male participants for the police officer sample. The age range for this group ran from 25 to 58 years of age with an average age of 40.6 years old. The educational levels ranged from some college to five participants with Masters Degrees. The years of service for the police officers ranged from one year to 31 years of experience as a police officer. The average years of experience was 16.2 years.

Table 1

Participant demographics for interviews held June and October 2017

African American Participants

Participant	Age	Gender	Highest Education
AA-001	36	Male	Associates
AA-002	71	Female	High School
AA-003	63	Female	1 Year College
AA-004	65	Female	High School
AA-005	71	Male	Associates

AA-006	68	Female	Bachelors
AA-007	72	Female	High School
AA-008	62	Male	High School
AA-009	41	Female	High School
AA-010	46	Female	Masters
AA-011	22	Male	Bachelors
AA-012	68	Female	Associates
AA-013	33	Male	High School
AA-014	72	Female	Associates
AA-015	31	Male	High School
AA-016	65	Male	Bachelors
AA-017	52	Male	Associates
AA-018	35	Male	Bachelors
AA-019	57	Female	Masters
AA-020	83	Female	Bachelors
AA-021	70	Female	Bachelors
AA-022	18	Male	High School
Average	54.6		

Police Officer Participants

Participant	Age	Gender	Highest Education	Years' Experience
PO-001	42	Male	Associates	19.5
PO-002	40	Male	Bachelors	16
PO-003	36	Male	Masters	15
PO-004	48	Male	Bachelors	22
PO-005	49	Male	Some College	25
PO-006	49	Male	Some College	27
PO-007	58	Male	Bachelors	31
PO-008	53	Male	Masters	27

PO-009	47	Male	Some College	25
PO-010	34	Male	Bachelors	10
PO-011	49	Male	Some College	25
PO-012	35	Male	Masters	8
PO-013	32	Male	Masters	5
PO-014	25	Female	Bachelors	3
PO-015	25	Male	Bachelors	1
PO-016	33	Female	Masters	3
PO-017	51	Female	Associates	25
PO-018	46	Male	Some College	25
PO-019	29	Female	Bachelors	3
PO-020	31	Male	Bachelors	8
Average	40.6	16.2		

Thematic Analysis Process

I conducted analysis for themes after interpretation of 13 questions asked in pre-post interviews with all 42 participants. Three questions were neglected on the part of the researcher due to error. Upon review of the transcripts, it was learned that three questions were not asked of the participants due to researcher oversight. Overall, there were 273 pages of transcribed interview data collected in this study. There were 13 questions asked of each participant group, which accumulates to 543 answers received during this process due to researcher error. I came to the conclusion that each question presented its own themes which needed further inquiry. Based on the questions and answers, I developed the themes through NVivo, assigning each answer to a code or node as it is called. I looked for common themes in answers to analyze the most common similarity in the answers. I looked at how African-Americans interpret police use of force incidents and how white police officers looked at marginalization. Prior to exploring these feelings, I looked at how each participant group felt about the topic.

After I coded the data for the themes, I met and compared the coded data from two Saint Mary's University inter-coder colleagues to compare our findings. It was found that our coding produced similar results. Using NVivo, we were able to determine our coding percentage agreement for each theme presented. According to Carletta (2008), having a matching agreement between inter-coder of 80% or higher is considered to have good reliability (p. 5). For this research, each theme will be assessed on its percentage for inter-coder reliability.

Many themes emerged from the data. The participants all had their individual opinions on this cultural dichotomy and how to improve it. There were few participants from both cultures who felt it was not their problem to solve and that the other needs to do more. There were others who were unsure what could be done to better solve this dichotomy. However, the great majority of participants wanted relations to improve. These participants were open to finding better ways of connecting and becoming mutual partners to these issues facing each other.

Many participants from both cultures also had eye-opening reactions during the simulated experience portion of this study. Participants questioned if the things they experienced really happened in the other's culture. Comments such as, "That really happens?" were heard over and over again. There truly were misunderstandings of what the other experienced during the course of an average day with many participants. Others were less believing of the experience, yet questioned their own thoughts and beliefs after the experience. There were some participants who felt the police can overcome difficult scenarios through training while others felt African-Americans could just ignore behaviors from unkind individuals. The expectations from some of these participants appeared to be a difficult task to overcome.

When the data were evaluated, it was apparent that both cultures by in large developed empathy and understanding for the other culture. Emotions are the universal language which can help people bridge their cultural differences and develop better understanding and interpretations (Shapiro & Gianakos, 2010, p. 24). There were emotional times during some of the interviews as participants developed different emotional reactions to what they just experienced. Having experienced for the first time what the other culture endures created mixed reactions and emotions during the interviews. From sadness to anger, these participants developed a better understanding of what each culture lives through.

In order to understand this dichotomy of how police use of force works and marginalization effects a certain segment of our community, I assessed all of the participants' views prior to the simulated experience of living in the others' culture. Analysis of these themes produced similarity in views from the two cultures, along with differences. I started the questioning in an attempt to assess how each group felt about their police department, its operations, its treatment of citizens, a general consensus of how African-Americans are treated across the country by the police, what could be done to make these relations improve, and their perception of how they have been treated in society. From these questions, five common themes emerged from the data with multiple sub-themes. These five themes were:

(1) The Wichita Police Department is looked at in a positive light by citizens and officers.
(2) African-Americans and police officers have opposite feelings towards enforcement actions and treatment of African-Americans.
(3) Similar opinions of how to make these relations improve.
(4) Similar feelings of how they feel they are treated.
(5) Police use of force and feelings on African-American crime.

There were four primary themes established with the African-American participants in the post-simulation experience. These four themes were:

(1) How surprised they were when it came to split-second decisions.
(2) Ethnicity played no role in decision-making to use force.
(3) Feelings of police work changes.
(4) Their experiences were realistic.

There were six primary themes established in the post-simulation experience with the police officer participants. These six themes were:

(1) This was realistic.

(2) Poor treatment.

(3) Wide ranging emotions were felt.

(4) Perceptions of the people in the scenarios.

(5) Will you treat others differently?

(6) Can you better empathize with people who are treated differently?

Pre-simulation Themes

What follows is a structural and textual discussion of how each culture viewed these themes.

Theme one: The Wichita Police Department viewed highly over-all by participants
The first theme that emerged from the data was the African-American and police officer participants generally held positive feelings toward their police department. Much of this positive feedback revolved around the change at the top with the new police chief, Gordon Ramsay, approximately two years earlier. The 22 African-Americans were asked how they felt the Wichita Police Department performed their duties. Twenty of these participants had positive comments about the job they were doing. Participant AA-001 stated, "Um, they doin' a lot. A lot of public engagement right now. There's a new police chief, so…I do see it there. They are makin' an effort to be more involved with the public."

AA-005 added, "Ah, right now with the police chief, I think they're doing pretty good. Ah just have ta…see what happens, but so far, it's better than it used to be."

AA-012 stated, "We have a good, a really good working relationship. um, we have a really great new police chief. I think they do really well."

AA-013 commented, "Um, ah, since the introduction of Chief Gordon Ramsay, I feel like there has been an improvement upon the Wichita Police Department in the way they perform their, their services."

AA-016 felt the department was "good to excellent." AA-018 felt "the Wichita Police Department does that job admirably."

AA-020 concluded, "I feel they perform exceptionally well. I don't see discrimination or any sort of acts of violence against another minority when they're doing their job."

There were two participants who had feelings that things could be better. AA-004 felt the police show too much force in common traffic stops, "If a person gets pulled over by the police for, ah, maybe speeding or no insurance or something like that, I don't see the need for it to be like…three or four police cars behind one car with flashin' lights and stuff goin'." As will be discussed later, these feelings changed in the post-simulation interview for this participant.

AA-020 had a different opinion on the job the Wichita Police were doing, "Not very well sometimes…because I just had an experience with them of someone breaking into my house. I called them, ah, and they didn't come, but they said they came later, much, much later but it was a rental and I didn't live there and I waited…I dunno, hours for them to come."

This negative view also was displayed when AA-020 commented, "Who had to pay for my door? I did. And I think something should be done about it. I think the people that broke in need to pay me for having my door fixed."

AA-002 was also mixed on how well Wichita police were performing their duties, "I would say a scale of one to five, if the scale is gonna be one to ten? I would give 'em a five. They still have a lot of work to do also."

Police treatment perspective

The police officer participants were asked if they feel they are treated fair from the public, their peers, and the administration. There were 15 out of 20 police officers who felt they are treated well for the most part. PO-003 responded, "From the public? I feel like, I feel like I've been treated fairly."

PO-004 added, "Yes. I believe I am."

Participant PO-005 qualified his answer, "Public and peers, yeah."

PO-007 stated, "I feel I am treated fairly, um, from all of the above."

PO-008 commented, "Any contact I have with citizens, whether I'm just out and about, I, it's usually really positive."

PO-009 felt, "Yes, I think, I think, ah, police officers here in this community are thought of and they're treated well by the community."

PO-013 quantified it, "Yeah, yeah, I'd say as a whole, ah, I'm treated fairly, ah, nine times out of ten."

There were several officers who did not feel they were treated fairly. There were six comments on how they felt the media is not treating them fairly.

PO-002 commented, "Maybe not so much in the media's eyes."

PO-006 added, "TV land and the media has really kind of put us at, we're not treated as well as I think, ah, as possible because of the media, social media, and mainstream both."

PO-010 felt, "It's just the latest trouble with the perception of police... especially with the media, it seems like it's more extreme."

PO-016 thought, "Just people recording things and the media...puttin' it on, but they don't have the whole story of everything."

PO-001 also commented on the media influence, "It depends on...media influence, which is, which I've seen through the years, depends on that."

Other police participants had different takes. PO-012 stated, "...from my experience, the good and the bad interactions tend to balance out, so there are definitely, ah, parts of the public who...ah, have a negative view of law enforcement and I feel, ah, don't treat us fairly."

PO-014 added, "It just depends...on who you come in contact with and their experiences with us, if they already have that set, mindset sometimes, right when they see the uniform, and...that usually, you know, who that is right when you get out of the car."

PO-018 specified more direct, "...I get treated as to what the public is seeing at that point, so if, if there's been a major incident that...law enforcement's looked at negatively then, in this community anyway, we will see our community react negatively towards us."

In summary, most participants felt the Wichita Police Department was doing a good job and the other treats them well in most situations. Most of the outliers were specific to other outside entities or specific incidents which affected their perspectives. The inter-coder reliability for this theme was 97% agreement for the AA participants and 96% for the PO participants.

Theme two: Opposing views on the treatment of African Americans

There were several questions asked from each group intended to see if African-Americans are treated differently by the police and what experiences created those beliefs. The African-American participants were asked if they believed African-Americans are treated differently by the police and if they felt they were ever targeted by the police based on the color of their skin. The police officer participants were asked if they felt African-Americans get targeted more frequently for enforcement actions by police officers and if Wichita police officers have bias enforcement towards minorities. The answers to these questions were polar opposite for these two groups.

The African-American participants overwhelmingly felt the police treat them differently. Twenty-one of the 22 had this opinion.

AA-001 opined, "Ah, yes, um, I think from what I've witnessed, um, I usually hang in a predominately white neighborhood, that's kind of where my hommies be at, ah, I have different homeboys, so when we're, when they kinda break up like a party…that's at, say we have a bonfire…ya know, whatever, they would come…oh God, ya know, I see you guys havin' a great time…ya know, you need to kinda keep the noise down, get some water on that fire, ya know… When they come to, we havin' a house party or a big cookout or something in the hood, it's, it's, it's…who's in charge here? You're gonna get a ticket, you guys need ta shut this down…this is ridiculous…and it's more of a…aggressive tone."

AA-002 felt it was more gender related, "I would say by gender. I think, um, there might be a gen, like they would mistreat a black male person more harshly than they would a black female person. I think it's gender."

AA-006 agreed, stating, "I think men are, are, ah, young boys are treated, treated differently, I really do."

AA-022 felt the police use, "More of a threatening tone, more of a…forceful way to get you to cooperate with them."

AA-003 stated, "I, I feel like, um, the police are afraid of black people in general."

AA-005 thought it was all based on power, "…white police officers they, they're young, and back then, like I was sayin', a lot of 'em just join…to get power, they have power and then they over emphasize their power."

AA-008 felt this way, "I mean...'cuz of the color, man, I mean, it's just, seem like...they wanna harass more of blacks than, ya know, they harass blacks."

AA-009 added, "I think it's a target to me, it's just a, I think it's just a target that, ya know, this is how African-American people are. Ya know?"

AA-013 added some research recently read on this subject, "...at least all the black people that I saw, that research was like, 'well, duh,' ya know, and it talked about how police officers talk to African-Americans differently than they do other people."

There was the feeling that personal bias affects how African-Americans are treated different. AA-013 stated, "I think it comes from the, ah, stereotypes that exists around African-Americans, um, ya know? Everybody is a little bit biased...ya know, um, and but it depends on if it's, ya know, um, and but it depends on if it's, ya know, explicit bias or, ya know, ah...um, or, or overt bias... um, everybody has bias."

AA-015, "I think, ya know, you have a lot of law enforcement that come from rural areas where there's not a high population of minorities in general and...what they believe a minority or black person or a Hispanic is is what they see on tv and a lot of times, we get those negative roles or criminal roles... and so they come into the situation assuming that because I'm a black man, no matter what I'm wearing, I'm up to no good at some point, and you get treated as such."

AA-017 added, "For one, I don't think they understand our culture. I think, you know, African-American people are a loud culture anyway."

AA-010 had a passionate answer, "Um, we went from a plantation of slavery to um...a systematic criminal based system that you want to call prison, um, to once again enslave people. We have a war on black people, which is documented by Nixon, um, incorporated that the black man is the biggest threat of the United States...shall I say of America...um, you have the war on drugs by Reagan, you have the Iran Contra scan by Reagan. You have the Oliver North hearing um, admitting that, ah, they brought guns into minority, ah, communities to have their guerilla warfare, ah, which has continued to this day. I don't give a damn what anybody says, you can't tell me Chicago keeps having, um, days where they collect 400 guns, the next week there's another 400 damn guns on the street. Where'd the guns comin' from?"

When asked if they ever felt they were targeted by the police, 15 of 22 reported they have not felt this.

AA-003 responded, "I'm thinking back...no, and I'll tell you why. My mother always told me to go the opposite direction of confusion."

AA-013 added, "I don't feel like I have ever been a targeted, ah, by the police based on the color of my skin. Ah, ya know, I, I, I obviously, ya, there's a, a really ingrained mistrust of the police though, through it's kind of woven throughout, ah, the African-American community." Twelve of the 15 simply responded "no" or "never experienced that."

There were seven participants who stated they personally have been targeted by the police based on their skin color, while three others stated they have observed others get targeted.

AA-001 stated he has experienced this multiple times, "...it wasn't in Wichita, it was in Virginia. Ah, basically they were doing a drug raid through all the neighborhoods at once, ah, I was visiting a family member's home. They didn't have drugs there, but we all came outside and then they all attacked us basically...in Houston, ah, I was walking from the store after I got off work... ah, due to the fact that the, ah, another corner store had gotten robbed, they, ah, said I fit the description...they took me to jail and booked me and all of that...and then, ah, basically told me 'you're lucky I'm doin' a thorough investigation or I's, well, just lock you up and throw away the key."

AA-015 experienced the following, "Um, let's see. There was a time I got pulled over on the highway, ah, by WPD and I had three other black people in my car. I drive a Monte Carlo, a '96 Monte Carlo...ah, I wasn't speeding 'cuz when I see law enforcement, I check to make sure I'm not speeding or doin' anything wrong....I asked him were we being detained? He said no...so I asked why he pulled us over and he said he just wanted to check on us and see how things were going...that's odd behavior from law enforcement."

AA-019 had this experience, "...when I asked him 'well, why'd you stop me?' He said, 'you were going 40 miles per hour. I said...I couldn't be goin' 40 miles an hour and his reply was, 'well, you're in a Mustang, you can do 40 miles an hour in a 30 mile an hour zone...and I'm like...no...at, at that point, I felt I had been targeted...so yes, I felt I was DWB."

AA-021 recalled a time back in the 1960's, "My husband was an outspoken person back in the 60's when he was livin', and um, in fact, he says he was targeted by the FBI, but um, ah, we had (inaudible) on 13th Street, ah, with the police chasin' us, ya know, but just goin' down the street, we had fights on Douglas Street, and ah, yeah."

AA-015 recalled a time when he observed police target a black man, "... there was a gentleman on a bike who, a black man, riding his bike, got surrounded by four officers and in a situation like that and these are four different police cars. Situation like that, I would assume you've done something worthy of you being arrested. And, and instead...they were getting loud with the gentleman, and when myself and four other people that were about a half block away started to walk towards the scene and they noticed us, they all got in their vehicles and drove off and then as we got up to the guy, we kinda ask him what was going on, and he said he's always getting harassed."

AA-019 recalled an incident 20 years prior, "I can remember this, since you brought it up, vividly, ah, a man getting cuffed and screaming at the top of his lungs, 'they're gonna beat me up."

Police participant's views
The police participants were asked if they thought African-Americans get targeted more frequently for enforcement actions by police officers in general and if Wichita police officers have bias enforcement towards minorities. Out of the 20 participants, 19 officers stated they did not believe African-Americans were targeted by the police for being African-American. Most of the officers qualified their beliefs based on crime, statistics, or location. Three officers stated they did think African-Americans were targeted, however, one stated this occurred in the 1960's.

PO-001 stated, "No because I just think, I think if you take all that, take... take all...skin color, cultures out of it, we're chasing the crimes."

PO-004 replied, "I have never arrested anybody that I did not feel was guilty of the crime being accused of."

PO-006 stated, "No, ah...do they, are they, blacks, my, no one is targeted in my experience. No one has been targeted. People might have felt like I was picking on them because I was writing parking tickets for people parking on their lawns, but what I was finding out was people were hiding dope in the cars, ya know, that were abandoned in the street, dope in the cars that were abandoned in lawns and stuff like that."

PO-008 commented, "I never really, never come across any, I mean, yeah, I occasionally stopped black people, but I also stopped white people or Hispanics or...it, ya know, it...whatever the violation was."

PO-009 added, "In our community, no. I do not."

PO-012 stated, "Um, I don't think so. Um, whether they're targeted unfairly for, for extra enforcement action, no. I don't believe that that happens."

PO-017 commented, "No. No. Um, I haven't seen it. So...um, and I've given a lot of thought to, had lots of time to think about it and have I seen it in my 25 years of law enforcement here in the city of Wichita, no."

PO-018 opined, "No, I don't think so. Ah, on, on a rare occasion, there's gonna to be a rouge officer out there that, that, that treats somebody a certain way because of who they are or what they are, but I, I don't and this is from my own personal opinion. I've never gone out there and said, 'I'm gonna arrest a, a Chinese person today' or 'I'm gonna arrest a black person today'...it doesn't...I mean, just, I don't see it from my law enforcement career at all."

PO-020 responded, "It's a hard question to answer. I don't think that they're necessarily targeted more frequently. I think that based on where we see our crime trends to occur and where we're seeing kind of our hots spots pop up...it's generally in lower income areas, some of our problem areas, and I think predominantly some of those areas are, population wise, are more predominately African-American."

Other police officers thought location was the reason behind these feelings as well.

PO-012 opined, "I guess to me that answer is, is complicated. Um, I think that...there is more crime, ah, in some areas of African-American communities, therefore there's a greater concentration of police officers in those communities...there are more 911 calls for police service ah, um, in African-

American communities, in some of them, and so, yes, there's more police action that occurs in African-American communities."

PO-010 added, "Parts of urban area that are more, ah, crime stricken are predominantly minority and of course, we're gonna put more officers into that area to try to remedy the living situation in that area. If crime is through the roof, yeah, more officers are gonna be there."

PO-006 replied, "Areas of town, ah, are targeted because of the crime that might be going on there."

PO-009 responded, "In our community, no. I do not...in general, across the country, I think they do."

PO-011 replied based on data, "I can say yes, and...I mean, I'm a data guy, too...and, ah, sometimes you hear things that, ah, you're like, 'wow' but you, you don't really, for whatever reason you don't think, something's not right, ok? Ah, so I think, um, as a percentage of population, yes. I think they do...I think black males are two and a half times more likely to be shot by police than white males or white people...and I believe that statistic, so, but I think you have to go a little bit deeper than that, but that's what people concentrate on... I can also tell you that, ah, a wa, police officer who is shot in the line of duty is more likely to be shot by a black man than a black man is to be shot by a white police officer...I rarely run across it with my fellow officer and it, those officers that show any sort of racism don't last very long and they get shunned by their peers."

In summary, these two cultures view the actions of the police very differently. The police feel their actions are based on crime trends and statistics, while the African-Americans mostly feel they are targeted based on ethnicity. This has become a primary divider in this dichotomy. The inter-coder reliability for this theme was 94% agreement for the AA participants and 98% for the PO participants.

Theme three: Making this relationship better
There were some very similar answers when both groups of participants were asked the same question: "What do you think can help develop better relationships in the African-American communities?" The two most common

themes with the African-American participants were more communication and more community policing. Community policing was mentioned by 13 of the 22 participants. Communication was mentioned in six of the 22 statements.

AA-001 mentioned the officers need to get into the schools more and get to know the kids better.

AA-001 stated, "I think it should be more engaged and actually goin' to each classroom and do a presentation where they have assemblies and like, ya know, we're here for you, this is the services we offer outside of this, ah, try to promote involved, ah, African-Americans get into the police force, cuz really, when you get home it's like, 'oh, Daddy been locked up for 18 years." AA-005 added, "…you might walk door to door…an' say 'hey…I'm officer so and so and just, how you doin' today? I'm just checkin' the neighborhood, makin' sure everything's alright' and…just, that's the way you talk to people."

AA-006 continued this thought by adding, "I think what would make better relationship with the, just to know the person. Or and to know, ah, people that are, are policing the area, ah, it can't be a, a us and them…it has to be a us."

AA-007 thought community engagement would also help, "Um, through, working through the churches and the community and getting things done, coming together in large groups, and I think that's a, that's really a plus."

AA-008 felt the police should set up booths in community areas for them to meet with citizens, "Ya know, ah, the community. Ah, and I know they're doing that now…comin' in and havin' a, little set-ups, ya know? Where people can know what, they can know people and people can know them more, ya know? That would be good."

AA-014 added, "I think community policing is exactly the tool. I know community policing is the tool. In other words, you know, either it be on their bikes or they're walking the neighborhood. There's National Night Out, and lemme tell you, we had one of the biggest National Night Out block party that there was."

AA-016 continued this theme, "Ah…more interaction, um, from a community involvement, ah, foot patrols, involvement with the community activities, ah, in African-American communities, to demonstrate that they are themselves human, the police are human just like African-American citizens are."

AA-018 added, "I think that's the first and biggest step, is building those relationships and being visible. Knowing, knowing who the residents are...knowing who the police officers are...and I, I don't think that this is a one sided police need to be doin' this...the community needs to do this as well...but I think the first step has to happen on the police side because there is a fear on the other side...so whenever you have someone who is in fear, you're not gonna, you can't expect the person who is in fear to make the first step."

AA-005 stated, "I mean, ya know, talk to the people, ask people and treat 'em as a person as you want to be treated."

AA-008 added, "Start, start, start comin' in and start talkin' to, communicatin' with 'em more." AA-009 continued this theme, "I feel like communicating, I feel like, um, them being present and showing that they do care, ya know, about situations...and not just, ya know, always just having an already stereotype...but I just think communication is the biggest thing, ya know, being more involved."

AA-011 stated, "Yeah, I think communication is key."

AA-012 added a key communication point, "Listening. Listening. You have to, you have to hear what, what's being said and take it as not just someone trying to get out of doing something or get out of complying, just listen to what they're saying."

Police agreement

When it came to the police officer participants, it was much more divided. Eight of the 20 mentioned community policing and seven mentioned communication. Another prevalent theme emerged from the police was six mentioned educating the public on police work would help build this relationship. Interestingly, training officers was only mentioned by three African-Americans participants and by two police officers.

Community policing was the most mentioned theme by the police officers.

PO-008 stated, "Community policing and getting with community groups, getting, ah, going to community meetings, working with neighborhoods, neighborhood associations, ah, was, was very beneficial because a lot of the community was tired of being victims of crimes or ah, ah, maybe there was shootings or maybe a drive-by in their neighborhood and they were tired of it, so workin' with them, they were willing to help us out and talk about a trouble residence or this house has got...ya know, traffic in and out of it, whether it's...maybe there's drug dealing or there's just kids hanging out...ya know, whatever it may be."

PO-013 added, "Just positive interactions, ah, police officers being able to spend time to attend community events or school events and stuff like that, I think really helps that relationship."

PO-014 referred to the cookout held by the police department in 2016. "...things like the cookout we had last year, that was like, and the chief really started that, a lot of people talked about it, so just showing up to more events, not acting like a, ya know, if that's your thing, we're gonna only go to certain events, um, and that kind of thing, like when there's little block parties, we always go and I think that really helps 'cuz it, a lot of the times you don't have time to get out of your car and go talk to people, but um, they really appreciate it most of the time...if we do that kind of thing."

PO-015 added, "Honestly? It, just more community time with them. Um, making the extra effort to go out and not just on calls, and go have community with these people...where you can actually go say 'hi' to them without having to go there for a 911 call."

PO-016 continued with this theme, "Well, I know we've had a lot of community functions. We had a cookout...and um, block parties and things like that where we try to get officers go and meet with the communities and stuff and it's worked pretty well I think."

PO-017 added, "Um, I think just being involved in the community, um, I know there's a lot of African-American people who are raised to just dislike the police, ah, or distrust, um, and so I just feel getting out there and ya know, 'hey, I'm a person, you're a person, I think there's a whole relationship that's not there...um, it's not...um, in a lot of homes, it's not taught to trust the police, it's taught the police are bad, um, and a lot of, um, African-American children grow up seeing bad things, police doing bad things in their homes or in the communities that, um, what, um, it looks like bad because, you know, they're arresting someone they know or something like that, so they grow up with the distrust and dislike."

PO-020 concluded, "I think the continual, the reaching out and try to gain that mutual understanding, um, I think it is a mutual respect that has to go both ways."

Another common theme came in the form of communication. PO-003 stated, "I think, again, it comes down to taking time to listen, I think it takes building that relationship and listening and not coming down and saying 'we're...we're not profiling...we're not doing this...but listen to what they're saying, listen to their side and take it into perspective."

PO-007 added, "I think much of what we have been working on for years, just trying to have people talk with the officers outside of an enforcement situation, ah, the problem I don't know how you deal with is so many of the people who are making the complaints, and I personally believe it's a fairly small number, relatively, ah, I don't know if there's anything you can do to convince them otherwise..."

PO-009 felt, "I think the open lines of communication and education, on both, ah, training such as possibly that can come from this, um, where we learn about each other's cultures, they learn about police culture and vice versa."

PO-018 concluded, "Um, communication. Educate the African-American community to what we do on a daily basis."

The theme of education also came up with six of the police officer participants.

PO-002 stated, "I think law enforcement has done a poor job in educating the community about, um, tactics and how, why we respond and how we respond and why shootings are justified...and we're not getting that information out to the community."

PO-013 added, "...education as far as...informing citizens what actual police officers do, how they do it, why they do it...ah, the day to day I think would be very helpful."

PO-020 added these thoughts, "...I think just getting back to them coming to the table and trying to understand how we do things as a law enforcement culture; why we do the things we do and then us understanding how they perceive it and some of their concerns on why we do the things we do…"

In summary, both participant groups had similar thoughts on how to make this relationship better. The primary themes came down to better communication and more community policing participation. The inter-coder reliability for this theme was 95% agreement for the AA participants and 95% for the PO participants.

Theme four: When I felt treated differently in a non-police setting
The literature review provided insight into a historical mistreatment of African-Americans in United States society. This experience has been seen and felt by many African-Americans during their lifetime. Looking to further the database, the question of ever experiencing marginalization was asked to the African-American participants. This semi-structured format also allowed these participants to cite specific incidents they have experienced throughout their lifetime. The theme was evident and strong for this question. Seventeen of the 22 participants could remember a time when this occurred. The police officers were asked a similar question. Their question was also based on their feelings of how they were treated. Their question was: "Have you ever been in a position where you felt you were not treated fairly outside of your police officer job?" Results from this question revealed 12 of the 20 participants have experience these feelings as well.

Here are a variety of times African-Americans have felt marginalized.

AA-001 states, "Ahaha! I get that all the time. But, um, mostly when I go down here to the courthouse, whatever, I, I have different visits, I'm tryin' ta fight for custody of my kids, stuff like that. Um, when you go through the security check, they give you, hass, they hassle me. Ya know, and it's only because…I believe because I'm black and I dress like this, or whatever, and they don't like, I don't think they like that."

AA-003 thought back in time, "Yes…I grew up in a point where, um…I'll say in, oh…when I was in the 7th grade. That was at a point when integration was just now coming forth. And I went to Coleman Junior High and I can tell the difference that was being made by the teachers, between a light complexed black person and a darker complexed person."

AA-004 brought up an example similar to one used for the police officer simulation experience, "...yeah, I have. Um, one time I went to a restaurant, it was me and this lady that I work with, and she was Caucasian...and the lady that waited on us...never acknowledged me as a person. She didn't even talk to me... while she was takin' our orders...and Mary told her, she said, 'Well, you see her sittin' there...why, how come you're not talkin' to her?' so that's one example."

AA-017 had a very similar experience, "Yes, in a restaurant. Me and my wife, this past year...went to a restaurant to eat...out west...and it was a place where you had ta be seated...ah, there was a couple before us that was seated... and everything, and no one ever came back to us...so, we seated ourselves. And no one came and acknowledged us, didn't come give a menu or water, so we got up and left."

AA-008 had a recent account of such treatment, "...oh ,yes!...Yes I, yes, I have. Well jus, well, just yesterday. I, I went to, I, I was up in (inaudible city name) and stopped at this convenience store and me and the guy who worked, we was in the line to go in the restroom, and this white guy came in, an' I told 'im, I said, well we's getting ready to go in the restroom, 'cuz he jumped in front of us, said, we was getting ready to go in the restroom next, and ah, he looked at me an' like, ya know, 'I don't care'...so his son walked off behind us and he told his son to come back up in front..."

AA-009 added a recent occurrence, "Yes...Um, I went into this, a store, a newly opened store, um, ya know, kind of expensive store and I, um, ya know, pep, they greeted people that came in and when me and another person went in, it was kind of...not as a greeting an' tellin' about the sales...like we just saw them tell the previous people that walked in...which were, ya know, older white women, and they didn't...ya know, give us the sales information."

AA-010 had more explicit memories of mistreatment, "Yeah...Um, I've been talked down to, I've been called ah, nigger by white people, I've been called apes by white people, I've been cussed out, um, I've been ah, potentially intimidated um, by white people just because I'm a woman, because I have brown skin, because I don't look like white people."

AA-013 commented, "Oh! Of course! Of course! Ah, yeah. I mean, there are situations where you go to the store and you have...ah...ya know, a white sales clerk that may follow you around, ya know, and I've had that ah, I, I'm the type of person, I, I, I seem to address those things…ya know, where, when they happen, ya know? Ah, you know and put that person on the spot."

AA-014 has also experienced this, "Yes, yes, I have…I felt like that, while shopping, if I was to go shopping at an exclusive, um, clothing store. I would feel that they were kind of…watching me more than they would maybe some of the white ladies or whatever within the store." These examples are similar to another simulation video the white police officers experienced.

There were also five African-American participants who stated they had never had the feeling of being treated different in their lifetime.

AA-002 stated: "Ah…no. I haven't ever experienced that."

AA-007 stated, "No. I'd say no." It is possible these five participants had simply not looked for unfair treatment, but they were adamant they have never felt marginalization.

Police: fair treatment

The police participants were also asked if there was a time as a civilian they thought they were not treated fairly. Twelve felt this on occasion, seven stated they never had this feeling, and two were unsure.

PO-001 remembered a time when he was younger, "…we were stopped by, ah, county deputy, and he, ya know, he searched us and everything like that and had a wad, I had a wad of cash on me…and immediately I was like, drilled, as, it's almost like, and I'm like, it, looking back I understand now."

PO-002 gave a different account, "…if I'm not dressed the right way and I'm wearin', ah, sweats and flip flops and a dirty shirt cuz I'm mowing the yard and I try ta go in a store to buy somethin', I notice…I don't get any attention…and no one, ones that talk to me, they don't think I have any money, so they treat me differently."

PO-012 had a different account, "Ah, sure…well, I can give you an example of when I felt I was treated unfairly by a police officer back when I was in college. I used to wear, ah, a bandana on my head, and I got stopped two or three times, and I was dead certain it was because I was wearing a, ah, bandana…I doubt that that's true…it's probably just because I was committing traffic violations, but I know I felt at the time that I was being targeted for that."

PO-014 experienced a different feeling of mistreatment, "Um, when I've been, I went to Walmart once and, um, I was buying, like, kitty litter and I had two big things, ya know, and I rang it up well, and she comes over and says, 'I saw you only rang up one'...not even asked, like 'can I see your receipt?' or anything...you only rang up one...and I'm like, really? Ya know, like, you can ask...there's a different way to put that, and no, I didn't...'oh, it's a computer error, but that was...ya know, I'm like, really...it seemed singled out, like she was trying to point a finger when it was...there's a different way to put it."

PO-017 has also had experiences where the treatment did not feel fair, "I mean, I, ok, this might be kind of silly, but it, it, it never fails, like, if my husband and I go out to eat or something like that, I always, he gets all of the service...and I really don't get any service when we have a female waitress."

PO-010 has had multiple experiences while dining out, "I know my wife and I, we've had a recent rash of, ah, going to restaurants and then nobody will...like wait on us...get a seat and then just...walk around us for...I think it was...45 minutes, we just stayed for fun, just to see how long it would take. There were other people that came in after us that got waited on, got their food and ah...that was, that's happened a couple times to us and one in particular, it was like, what is going on?" Since this participant has had this occur on more than one occasion, you can guess it had little effect when he viewed a video identical to this during the simulation part of this research project.

There were seven police officers that really could not come up with a specific incident.

PO-019 commented, "Oh, I mean, I think life's not fair and that happens to everyone, I, I mean there's lots of, in school and growing up and stuff, yeah. Not, not everything is fair."

While PO-020 did not have a specific example, this was stated, "I think general rudeness, I mean, being out and about, um, you go down into like our old town, into the bar section, and you'll have people cuss at you, ah, I've been called privileged just because I'm white."

In summary, the distinction between marginalization and feeling mistreated had different meanings for the participants. More African-American participants felt marginalization than police officers felt being a victim to bad treatment. There were, however, participants from both groups who stated they have not experienced this phenomenon. The inter-coder reliability for this theme was 95% agreement for the AA participants and 97% for the PO participants.

Theme five: Police use of force/African Americans commit more crime?

The participants in this research study were asked several questions to determine how they felt about police use of force and African-American crime beliefs. The African-American participants were asked for their beliefs as to whether the police use too much force and if they have ever seen abusive behavior by the police. These specific questions were: Do you believe the police use too much force? Have you ever been assaulted, abused, or observed abusive behavior by the police on other African-Americans? The police participants were asked: Do you believe police officers in general think African-Americans commit more crimes? The objective here was to understand how these participants felt about police use of force before experiencing the simulation exercise themselves. The police participants were asked a general question to gauge how they felt police officers in general felt about African-American crime perceptions to determine if there was bias occurring among police officers in general.

The themes drawn from these questions produced some interesting answers. Eighteen of the 22 African-American participants believed the police use too much force at least some of the time, yet 15 of the 22 stated they have never been abused or observed abusive police behavior or were unsure if they had. There were seven who stated they have experienced it or heard of others experiencing police abuse. When it came to the police officers' perspective, the answers were more evenly dispersed. Eleven of the 20 participants thought police officers in general think African-Americans commit more crimes, while nine felt officers do not believe African-Americans commit more crimes or were unsure.

When it came to African-Americans' perceptions on police use of force, here are some of their responses.

AA-001 stated, "Ye, yes. Um, because I, I was, I was, um, in Virginia when, um, when the Tasers came out and this musta been, ah, a non-lethal way of subduing a suspect, stuff like that...but I know, well, what I, my perspective, when the tasers came out, they started usin' their guns more...'cuz before the tasers came out, you hear about a police shooting, ya know, once a month, it'd been in different parts of the country, and now I'm hearin' about it like, four or five times a month an, in, in same states, you know what I'm sayin?"

AA-003 added, "Yes, I do. There's some situations, um...you don't have to shoot to kill...especially when you see a person's already down...there's no reason for you to go, go over there and chomp on 'im and jump on 'im."

AA-010 opines, "Yes. Um, I guess that's the million dollar question, why do they use so much? Ah, reactive force? Um I...I think the information that is given to them, um, isn't researched, the, the people providing the information to the 911 dispatcher, who's providing the information to the police officer, um, that information is not validated, um, so they have a certain mindset, ah, that's already heightened, um, because that's kind of on the level that that's their job but misinformation, um, creates a bad situation."

AA-012 continues, "Nationwide, yes. I, if, you need to listen when you go to a call or situation, you need to have more information, so that ya know, we have a lot of mental illness now."

AA-015 had this perspective, "Yeah. Ya know, I just value life a little more than that. Um, I think in certain situations, you can de-escalate verbally. There are some where more force is necessary, but I think often times, they jump the gun too quick and I dunno if that's a cultural deal or a societal deal, but just think, ya know, you, you know you have a weapon that can kill someone...and I guess fully protect you, but at the same time, we don't care about the life of the person that we're interacting with."

AA-018 contends, "Yes. I think the level of force used, I think the level of force used in a lot of situations comes too early. I think that, while I understand the life and death instances that happen, and that within a blink of an eye, everything can go bad and that their human and just anyone else...I believe sometimes the overuse of force gets to be more adrenaline based than necessary based."

AA-021 contends, "I do. I do and feel that it's just…I think because, um, they have a lot going on in North Carolina…I was there for a month and a half…and…seemed like anything that involved a black person, you get shot."

Some of these participants were unsure if the police use too much force.

AA-005 stated, "Back in the 80's, maybe early 90's…yeah, they, sometimes they used too much force."

AA-008 added, "…I feel like they, ya know, don't have to kill, you know, a person. I…hurt his leg, shoot him in the leg or in the arm…or something."

AA-011 was indecisive, "That's a hard one to answer. I mean, a part of me says yes…but sometimes no. 'Cuz some of the things they have to deal with."

AA-019 was also uncertain, "In general. It depends. It depends on the situation. Ah, yes and no. Sometimes I believe they use too much force when you end up dead for what should have been a ticket…and then sometimes I think they don't use enough force…because they are afraid that if they use the force, they will be called, ah…certain names."

Others did not believe the police used too much force. AA-007 surmised, "…I really can't say because, unless I see something on the media, to warrant that? And I haven't seen anything recently on the media to, to say that they do."

AA-014 agreed, "Now. There you go, ok. And when you look at the present, of the, the, what's going on now as the present, here and I'm thinking about my surrounding, I don't think so…from, from my experience of what I've been in. I don't, I don't, I don't think so."

When it came to witnessing abusive police behavior, the majority stated they had not observed this. AA-003 reflected. "Yeah, I'm, I'm thinking back… no, and I'll tell you why. My mother always told me to go the opposite direction of confusion, it's just been here lately that I've, um, been more active, ya know, but ah, when I was younger, no."

AA-008 followed this thought, "I…nah, no. I mean, I, I always been a loner. I never been around a lot of people…if I do see, ah, things going on, I always turn and go another way. Yes, so I just…ya know, I try to avoid that type of stuff."

AA-020 hypothesized, "No...I haven't...I haven't...witnessed anybody being abused...firsthand. Perhaps because I'm not out there to...you know, see the event take place." AA-005 added, "Ah...no, not really. No, unless they deserved it, I mean...sometimes you get outta hand, so you have to use force."

There were six participants who claimed they have witnessed police abuse firsthand.

AA-001 recounted, "I've, um, well, we had a parade, we had, ah, a block party in Virginia. Me and my uncle were walking to the store 'cuz the block party was already goin' on, I was waitin' for him to get off of work, he got off, we walked from my house, it's the top of the street to the corner store, and it was so many people in the street, so the police are like, ya know, 'you guys gotta get out of the street'...'cuz they are doin' something and so we were all trying ta get on the sidewalk, but there was so many people, we were kinda getting bumped back into the street, so he walks up to my uncle, he's like, 'you need to get on the sidewalk'...he's like, 'sir, I can't get on the sidewalk'...and he punches 'im and knocks him on the ground."

AA-013 contended, "Um, yes. I, I have seen...um, yeah, I have seen, ah, police officers, ah, um, at least act aggressively towards people. Um, or, or, or question, ah, people, ah, very aggressively...ah, I haven't actually witnessed someone actually being physically, ah, assaulted...Um, it, it's, it's just, it was always just, ah, like verbal."

AA-018 recalled, "Ah, we were held on the ground for an hour and a half, 45 of those minutes with SWAT team holding guns at us...pff, ah, and then with the wire cuffs...the, this, some of this is probably emotional as much as it is, ah, physical. Ah, when they were struggling to get the wired handcuffs off of us, ah, they were making jokes about, 'well, do you think he could drive home anyway?' Um, they couldn't figure out how to take them off, so then they were like, 'ah...well, maybe you'll just have to stay like this, I'm sure it won't be a problem."

AA-021 recalled, "Only in the 60's. I haven't, yes, I haven't observed anything like that now."

Do African Americans commit more crimes?

The majority of police participants felt officers in general thought African-Americans commit more crime. Here is how some of them defended that claim.

PO-001 stated, "Yeah. Yeah, I do believe that. I believe base, based off of just what we deal with day in and day out. You listen to music, you listen to the, and I, and I, I will but it has ta, it kind of pushes that culture, pushes that culture to be, ah, to get into those things, ya know, 'money over bitches' type songs, ah…'ridin dirty'…all of these different things that kinda point to and you…you get that…within the African-American community."

PO-004 added, "I think as a whole, I, yeah, I think we do."

PO-006 continues this thought, "Yeah, I would, I would say that's, that's a, a fair perception. Ah, and ah, not yeah, I would. I would say that some, some could think that, that, that's possible."

Others backed this contention with statistics. PO-007 stated, "Statistically, ya know, per capita, ah, based on percentages of how many whites, blacks, Hispanics there are, I think they feel that the African-Americans are more likely to commit a crime based on the smaller population than the, if you compare it to the same population of whites."

PO-011 postulated, "In that, the data in the study shows that in the 75, I believe it was, biggest counties in the United States, I think it was, ah, black males committed 55% of robberies, they committed almost 60% of the murders, and 45% of the assaults, but within those 75 counties, the minorities make up only 15% of the population."

PO-012 added this perception, "I think that, that would have to do with, um, personal experiences at least of the officers I work with in this bureau, um, sits right in the middle of an African-American neighborhood, um, so the vast majority of the work that we do is with African-Americans…and so that effects perception."

PO-018 also reflected on statistics, "I think police officers can see the data…and I think police officers see the numbers that the general public doesn't see…and I think the police officers realize that the size of the population that as, that African-Americans have in most communities, they realize that African-Americans are involved in more crime, not that they commit the majority of crime. But that African-Americans, for the size of population in most areas, are involved in a higher number of crimes than any other minority group, I would say."

There were a large portion of these participants who did not feel the same way.

PO-002 opined, "More white people commit more crimes, I think all law enforcement officers would know, know that, but per capa, if you looked at a percentage of the groups, then you would see, ah, the African-Americans commit more crimes within their African-American culture verses other groups because of social economic issues."

PO-003 added, "I, I don't think so. There's not, to me there's not a perception that only African-Americans are committing these crimes. It's, it's, there's crimes across the, across the board." PO-008 contended, "I don't really believe that, I don't have any one of my troops here, sittin' here, and say… they target one, they say anything about race, committing crimes."

PO-009 theorized, "I don't think they believe they commit more crimes. I think, ah, just the nature of the crime that they com, that they commit, which it seems to be more, ah, person crimes more than property crimes. They're are brought to the limelight more because they're, the violent actions, the violent natures…of them. I think the, the way the media portrays it is very much the way and social media itself I think has heightened it…and has portrayed it, ah, and given the perception of it."

PO-020 contended, "I don't think so. I know…that it is not, it's not really a conversation I've ever had with any officer or anything that I've heard voiced, ah, from many of the officers that I talk to, so it's, it's a hard one to answer."

PO-014 was unsure, "In general, I would say it goes 50/50, I don't know, I…it depends on your beat really, if you see it all the time, it tends to be like, that's all you're around, ya know, so um, I mean, to be honest, it just depends. If you go out, ya know, on Rock Road, it's pretty much white people committing the crimes, so it just depends on what you're around."

In summary, this theme had differing opinions within each participant group and between the two groups. The consensus with the African-American participants was that the police do use too much force, however, only a small portion have personally witnessed this occur. The police participants were divided when it came to the belief that African-Americans commit more crimes. The inter-coder reliability for this theme was 98% agreement for the AA participants and 97% for the PO participants.

African-American Post-simulation themes

The participants were given six video scenarios apiece upon conclusion of the first set of interview questions. After these six scenarios finished, the participants were each asked six follow-up questions about their experiences in the simulation exercise. These questions were formatted to gauge the effects the video scenarios had on the participant's perceptions of the experience and if these experiences changed their beliefs. Only two of these questions were similar in nature to each participant group. For this reason, there were many more themes and sub-themes developed in the data. The following are the African-American themes most viewed by the participants.

(1) How surprised they were when it came to split-second decisions.
(2) Ethnicity played no role in decision-making to use force.
(3) Feeling of police work changes.
(4) Their experiences were realistic.

Theme One: Surprised on split-second decision making
When it came to experiencing simulated use of force scenarios, the participant's words reflected an overwhelming surprise in how quickly use of force can occur in police situations. There were two questions related to this theme: "What is your perception of police use of force after experiencing Laser Shot? Do you believe it is hard to make critical decisions in split-second time? Why? Twenty of the 22 participants stated they did think it was difficult. Twelve of the participants also commented on how surprised they were with the scenarios after the experience. The two who did not think it was difficult made these comments.

AA-006 stated, "…only if you are not trained. If you're not trained for it, yes. If you are…are trained for it, um, you can, from your intuition…and experience and practice, you can make, ah, ah, judgements, ya know, a quick decision on things like that."

AA-015 added, "If you're prepared, no. But if not, then ya, it is."

Thirteen of the 22 participants make specific comments about quick decision making when asked on the first question about their perceptions of police use of force. Twelve also commented they had more understanding of the job of a police officer now.

AA-001 thought, "I think it's more of a judgement call because, um, since each, each situation is kinda in a spur of the moment, then it would draw on you to kind of rely on yourself and your reactions."

AA-002 added, "So, what would be difficult in a split second, in my opinion. You have to make split-second decisions whether to be violent, non-violent to protect or not protect, you have a lot of things you have to experience before you…really react."

AA-003 contended, "Ah…my perception was…it is very easy to jump the gun. If you don't…slow enough and observe the whole situation, um…you have to be calm but alert in all situations 'cuz it just takes a half a second to make wrong decisions, wrong…mistakes, yeah."

AA-005 opined, "Oh, ok. It's…it's a good simulator. It did make you think…and then, ah…this, a of different situations, ya know? 'Cuz a lot was on split seconds."

AA-007 thought, "Yeah because those scenarios really make you realize the danger that the officers are in could be on a daily basis…and if you make just a split decision anticipating trouble…it could save your life or you could take another life…but you're only doing your job." AA-008 added, "Yeah, 'cuz I mean, just lookin' at that…I mean, things happen so fast. Ya know, and I know they, they get trained for this, but I mean…it happens so fast. You have ta be alert of everything. If you ain't, you can be gone…yeah."

AA-009 was surprise, "Wow! It…it makes me think…'cuz things happen so quickly. Like in a matter of seconds…so the protection of thereselves…it's very important. I mean…not knowing what a person will do…from one second to the next."

AA-014 justified things, "Because let me tell you, and you have to think (snap of her fingers) in a split second for your life and your back-up, your partner, plus the people around you, too! After seeing that, I, I, I, I, I, I, I can see where, if a police use excessive force, ah, ah, and make a mistake, I, I, I, I, I, I could, I could justify it and see why and how."

AA-018 added, "Ah...I think that, I mean, use of force is, ah, like is very tough to gauge...and ya know, in a blink of an eye...you don't know when the situation's gonna turn, and I think that was evident in this, in the role play."

AA-004 was surprised, "Yes! Because I saw things in the scenarios that I was not expectin'. I saw what, two people get shot and myself, and I did not see that coming!"

AA-010 stated, "Oh, yes, yeah, um, I, I, I honestly think, um, it requires a lot of training...maybe more than nine months' worth of training...um, because we have a lot of psychological collateral damage that nowadays people bring to them, to an argument or in a road rage, ah, or in domestic violence case...there's some sort of mental illness, um, that's not been addressed, diagnosed...treated...things like that, that brings a lot of these cases, um, to the spotlight."

Other participants developed more understanding of the roles of police officers.

AA-012 stated, "Um, I guess some of that is justified? Whhh, but I, some of that is justified I would assume, just, but the deadly part I have an issue with...that you would...hopefully deescalate the situation with? So, yeah, I guess I can see why deadly force is, is used."

AA-016 surmised, "Um...I can see why force would be, ah, is an option that is...more prevalent today than one would expect due to what I just seen. I can see that they would option to do that more."

AA-017 felt, "Ah...I still think...it's...I think they should use it when they have to. I don't think it should be used all the time. I didn't use it when I needed to (laugh)."

AA-021 seemed perplexed, "I'm still against it, (sigh) but I can see where you might have to use force, but...don't jump just because you think somebody might have a gun...but if you wait until you see it, it's too late! So, this is a hard question. Wow! I don't want to say I'm for it...(laugh)." AA-022 thought, "That necessary force is necessary, sometimes you have to watch a situation closely, make sure that there's no-one agitating, walking around, and if there is, then reaching for your gun is an option."

In summary, these participants overwhelmingly thought split-second decisions in use of force scenarios were difficult. Participants experienced through simulation how quickly things change in police use of force incidents. It had an eye-opening effect to many participants. The inter-coder reliability for this theme was 96% agreement.

Theme Two: Ethnicity was not a factor in decisions to use force
When asked if the suspect's ethnicity ever played a role in their decision to use force, all 22 participants stated it did not ever play a factor.

AA-001 stated, "No. Ah, my, my, ah, choice of force would have been based on the threat. Um, I, ok, I'm thinking back, the African-American lady had mental problems...she had a stick...never really seen the African-American lady, just seen a person with mental diseases with a stick."

AA-002 added, "I was lookin' at the, the situation. Rrrr, race, color, gender, never even came to my perspective. I was just looking at the situation."

AA-003 reflected, "I didn't even see it! Okay? My life was on the line! And you're doin' somethin'...ah...this is if you didn't hear the orders that I gave you...I didn't see no color. I really didn't. Bein' honest with you. I'm dealing with the situation at hand."

AA-004 was adamant, "No. No! No. It was just the situation. No, un-huh. Un-huh. Un-huh. And to me, that's how it should be."

AA-008 also responded with passion, "Oh, no! No! No! No, I didn't. Not one time. Not at all. No, it didn't. Not at all. If, ah, no, race didn't come in at all."

AA-009 replied, "I....I really didn't. I didn't even...think, 'oh...this is a, this person, or ya know, this race or this culture...and I didn't even pay, I, I mean...I, I know the last lady was a, ya know, an African-American lady, but the other ones...I mean, that didn't even cross my mind, and say, oh...this was a black man, so let me shoot...or lemme pepper spray or let me tase...it, I just, just was watchin' what was going on."

Referring to the last lady in the videos, she was actually of Hispanic decent, which helps back-up the claim that ethnicity was not looked at closely by these participants.

AA-010 also had a problem remembering the ethnicity of people encountered, "No, I never even thought about it. I never...I thought about the man being drunk on the couch was a drunk man on the couch. I never thought about, ah, if he was white or Mexican...that, I don't even know if he was white or Mexican."

AA-012 postulated, "No. No. Right is right, wrong is wrong. If you're in the wrong, then...that's why you, why we call the police because somebody's in the wrong. Color has nothing to do with that. Wrong is every color."

AA-015 assumed, "So, in that sense, yep, gender might have played a part in assuming nothing would happen like that."

During one scenario, a female grabbed a gun during an argument and shot another female. This participant, AA-015 seemed surprised this could occur and never pulled his firearm out to defend himself.

In summary, none of these participants stated the ethnicity of the suspects they dealt with in the simulated scenarios played a role in their decisions to use force. In today's society, it becomes easy to assume ethnicity plays a role in police officer involved use of force scenarios, however, this did not occur with these simulations. The inter-coder reliability for this theme was 98% agreement.

Theme Three: Feelings about police work changes

Nine of the 22 participants did not change their opinion on police work or were somewhat changed from the experience. Thirteen felt they had changed their views of police work.

AA-001 speculated, "Nnn, no. Not really. 'Cuz I think they still gonna have ta make the same judgement calls, so...I dunno, I've never been through actual police training, so I'm thinkin' that is some element of the training that would have you being able to deal with situations like this, to a certain extent."

AA-005 added, "No, I kinda know how it works...it's...yeah, they got a hard job."

AA-013 contended, "Um...no. Ya know, I, I again, no. I don't think that, that it made, makes a difference."

AA-015 opined, "Not really. Um and maybe I'm the wrong person to ask that, again, I work in corrections and plus I've been workin' on community law enforcement relations, too, so, I kinda seen, we all step up for the position."

AA-018 opined, "No, they did not change. I...I understand the level of... ah...I understand the level of concentration, I understand the level of fear that has to go into doing this job. I don't understand, I don't understand the job fully 'cuz I don't do it every day, but I understand, I can understand, ah, and not just relate to un, the understanding of not wanting to be in danger and wantin' to make sure you see your, to get home safe, I can, I can totally understand that, um...the use of force is always gonna be something that's...kind of, gonna be an iffy situation."

There were 13 participants who had different views. These participants did have changed feelings about police work.

AA-003 responded, "Oh, yeah. Ah...I got a lot, a greater respect for 'em, I mean, I already had respect for 'em, but I have a greater respect for 'em now because, ah...(long pause) (she's emotional as she continues to talk)...you don't realize how much they put their lives on the line, they have a family to go home to...and we always, we're so quick to blame 'em for everything, you know? We don't take accountability...our responsibility for our actions. And I'm not talkin' about me, per se...but people in general."

AA-004 stated, "Yes. I haven't really experienced anything...I mean, for me....My, you know, 'cuz the only thing that they've, that a police officer's ever done to me is give me a ticket...but as far as anything critical like....the scenarios...I've never experienced that. To me now. The police, they have to do what they have to do...and I understand now why they have more than one police officer on the scene sometimes...for back up...and it's scary to me."

AA-006 added, "Because I understand now the...ah...the adrenalin danger...the danger that you can face from, ah, irrational citizens and each, each, ah, especially if you're, if a policeman is called, ah, so my, ah, perception just from this video and things like that are really, I really can, ah, understand why it's not a, a...finger on the trigger thing."

AA-007 thought, "Yes. Because realizing…those scenarios, this could happen regular on a daily basis. And a split decision may not be the best decision, but you're doing the best you can."

AA-008 felt, "Yes, it changed. I mean, yes, it has…it changed…that…people have, peep, you have to, they have to be ready. They, the change from be protecting you or just like the, like the, ah, man jumped on his wife, you know, you have to be ready for anything at a split second, you just have to be ready, man. I mean, I can't explain, you know, what I was seein', I know I was standing there (laugh) but you have to be ready for anything and it made me change that they were doin' their job…and people can…they get shot or, ya know, they have to protect themselves all the time."

AA-009 contended, "Yes, a little bit. It did. I guess I keep saying the same thing. Because you just don't know, you just don't know from one second to the next what that person is capable of doing. And so…their work is…is so…um…critical. It's so important. Or so…it could be deadly, in, in a second!"

AA-011 added, "Yes. Un, more understanding that their job is pretty difficult and sometimes some of things they have to do is split-second life or death decisions."

AA-012 opined, "It's making me think. I've always thought you could maybe just deescalate the situation, but I, after doing this scenario…there, probably some situations that you're just not gonna be able to do…and you're gonna have to look at, um, whether or not you walk away from the situation."

AA-014 gained support, "After going through this, I would support the police even more, what they have to go through and what I was feelin' myself and my body, and they're human, too! And they have families, too! And I'm thinkin' about the, the adrenaline and, and, and the, oh the, the thinkin' that you have to do. Yeah."

AA-016 experienced, "Yes. Uh, again, more empathy toward police, ah, hap, leaning, what we see in the media or experience that have, of people using force more because of the seemingly aggressiveness of the…environment that they work in, the violence in the environment they work in."

AA-019 had similar thoughts, "I have more empathy for what they have to do. I could not be a cop. Really, I, I, too much stress. Too much stress 'cuz you're on 12 all the time. Every time you get a call, you're on 12. If stress is one to ten…As a cop, you're on 12."

AA-021 was a little effected, "…(sigh) five percent. I'm still going to say they pull out their guns too soon…ah…they shoot when they should tase. I'm still be critical…I'm, I, I, I can see sometimes when they…ah…ah, put in a situation like this…but then I'm gonna say…um, when he went to the car with, on that woman…that it was, if it was a black woman, he woulda had his gun already. That's what I'm gonna say."

AA-022 concluded, "A little bit, yes. I know that they go through situations like this, a lot of the times…and that necessary force is necessary sometimes…and I see that now, that it's more necessary than it is not necessary."

In summary, many of the participants stated their feelings changed about police work in a positive way from this experience. Two participants mentioned they gained more empathy for the police after their experience. In afterthought, these post-simulation questions should have asked a specific question related to empathy as it did with the police participants to gain new knowledge. However, through the participant's words, this can be measured through their answers. The inter-coder reliability for this theme was 96% agreement.

Theme Four: This was realistic

There was an overwhelming amount of positive answers when the participants were asked if their experience was realistic. Twenty-one of the African-Americans commented on the experience as being realistic.

AA-001 commented, "It is realistic. It is very realistic and it, it happens often the unknowns are so widespread, you don't know if people are on drugs, or like her, like she coulda been how, how, hell, high, high-end or whatever."

AA-004 added, "Very! Because like I said…I saw things that I, that I didn't see coming and it's, ya know, when you're goin' to a situation it…I saw things that I was not expecting to see. Things that happened that I wasn't expecting to happen…'cuz I couldn't see it comin'…so they have to be…just read, like you said, ready with split-second decisions. They have to be."

AA-006 claimed, "Very! It was so realistic, I screamed!"

AA-007 postulated, "Yes. Because those just, average, those are the average people in the day to day routine…um…and we don't know what…so many people using drugs now, we just don't know what type of situation they're in and how their perception is at different times and some of them are out driving…and making…difficult movements, which would maybe engage an officer to stop them because they're doing something incorrectly, so…with this being said, anything can happen if you're stopped by a police officer."

AA-010 posited, "Oh, yeah! I mean, if you, if you get on the news, if you listen to the radio, you could probably watch one or two of these scenarios, simulator videos in real life. On Facebook Live."

AA-012 concluded, "Oh, yes! I, as an observer…I, I…it was shocking to me how quickly it went from good to really bad and how deceptive some people are. It, that…I will admit, totally surprised me how quickly it, it went."

AA-016 experienced this, "Yes, yes. 'Cuz it looked at a variety of situations that I could personally be involved with, situations that again, you hear reiterated in the media, ah, that, that showed me these do exist and, um, my…mental involvement with it, which showed that I, I have a, ah, of course without training…I have a, a, ah, problem with making the decision with the experiences that I went through. So, I can, again, can have empathy toward why they would probably, there are more issues with the policing, why we have more incidents of others having struggle with making that decision, even though they're trained."

AA-017 replied, "Yeah. It was really having my adrenaline pumpin'! So, yeah, ah, it, it was…it was interesting to, ya know, put yourself in the positions at times, and ah, know that you have a split-second…to make a decision to either save your life or save someone else's life."

AA-013 had a different opinion, "Um…yes and no. When you're doing things on a video…ya know, my heart rate is not gonna be the same, my adrenaline…is, is not gonna be the, the same, ya know, this, ah, my, the physiology, ya know, is, is not at, at all the same. The physical response is, is not a, the same as, as the, a lived real world experience if you automatically kind of have the perception, and I did, that you're not gonna be hurt…in the situation."

In summary, the participant's over-all felt the simulated experience was a realistic experience for them as it pertains to living as a police officer. Their understanding of how police use of force is a rapidly changing event altered some of their pre-scenario perceptions. While these participants were not specifically asked if they had more empathy for the police after their experiences, through their words conclusions can be drawn that they did. The inter-coder reliability for this theme was 95% agreement.

Police Post-simulation themes

The police participants went through the same process as the African-American participants. After their six scenarios, they were asked six follow-up questions about the experience. Through their transcripts the following themes came into focus. (1) This was realistic. (2) Poor treatment. (3) Wide ranging emotions were felt. (4) Perceptions of the people in the scenarios. (5) Will you treat others differently? (6) Can you better empathize with people who are treated differently?

Theme One: This was realistic

The majority of police officer participants commented that their experience was realistic. Seventeen of the 20 officers stated so.

PO-004 stated, "Was it effective showing me that people believe they're picked on because of their race or their age? Or their sex? It is effective. I do, the gentleman, my buddy in the, walking down the street, my buddy at the state fair…they were, they do believe that they were fol, he does believe he was followed because of his race. That's very clear to me. Was…was he followed because of his race by the officers? I can't see any other reason why. I looked, I was lookin' at everybody around, there were no other black people there at all, everybody's, all the law enforcement's concentrating on him, yeah. It, I can't equate it to anything else."

PO-007 added, "Ah, like I say, listening to my friend in the two scenarios, the black gentleman, helped me maybe to understand a little more where he's coming from. Like I said, doesn't matter if it's right or wrong, but that's where he is coming from."

PO-010 opined, "I…mean, it opened my eyes and I've always been a skeptic to the diversity, well, I've attended some pretty poor, ah, 'why cops are racist training' where it was a four-hour lecture...by some people that obviously had an agenda that were let in the room for some reason, and so, yeah, this is good. This is good, especially with the studies have shown that this happens to black people. You're like, 'okay, there's data behind it'...and I don't want to say it makes it more believable, 'cuz I know these things happen."

PO-012 added, "It's still necessary to understand the full picture but this is, this is a common experience of a, of a huge portion of the American public that experiences this on a daily basis, and so, yes, I think it is a very good thing, ah, to go through this type of thing."

PO-015 posited, "I believe so. I believe so. Ah, it definitely gets you to see, in the eyes of other people, um, and see how people are being treated unfairly...um, and experience cultures that you're not a part of."

PO-019 commented, "Realistic, yes, um, ya know, I think it all depends on if people are open minded or not, um, I think that there's a lot of us who would be open to seeing this and, ya know, open to changing our minds and then probably, ya know, half of the populations just says, 'oh, this stuff isn't an issue'."

PO-020 concluded, "I think it was pretty realistic. Ah, I mean, it got, it definitely got the point across and the concepts across for the issues."

In summary, the majority of the police participants felt their experience with the simulated scenarios was realistic. The consensus from these participants indicated these participants understood the messages of the videos and felt they were witnessing these events as they viewed them. The inter-coder reliability for this theme was 96% agreement.

Theme Two: Poor treatment

All 20 police participants made comments that during at least one point in the videos, they felt they were not treated fairly or an actor was not treated fairly. However, there were also 11 who made comments that attempted to justify what happened or simply did not think they were treated badly in some of the video scenarios.

PO-002 stated, "In some they were, and it could have been, for some they weren't. One of the scenarios, the second one, I think it was the jewelry store one, ah, that was a little odd, because ha, ya know, all the guy had ta do is hand her an application and…run her credit, an she…she, there's no reason to hassle her about her finances and everything…".

PO-004 opined, "The first one, yeah. I mean, those cops were following me…ah…the ah, restaurant, that's just really bad service, and was it because of who I was? I have no idea. Ah…the jewelry store? Yeah, I was treated unfairly. I…didn't feel like I could equate, ah, all, I don't know why I was treated unfairly to…in some of them."

PO-007 wavered, "Nnn, not in well, it wasn't so much that I wasn't treated fairly, but I don't think my niece was treated fairly at the jewelry store, ah, I don't know what the customs guy's issue was, so I don't know if I was treated fairly or not there, I didn't really have a feeling one way or another. The restaurant I…I donno about fairly, ah, I don't know why they wouldn't serve us, wait on us but, ah, so other than the jewelry store, I…I didn't get a feeling of being treated unfairly but…my wife would tell you…I don't tend to really let things like that get to me that much."

PO-008 continued, "Well, it depends on which one. The one with the… the airport? No. 'Cuz I'm like…ya know? I didn't, I didn't feel like I was being treated fairly there, in the airport scenario. Um, my friend at the county fair? The problem was, the target was on him, er, not sayin' target, but the issue was with him, the way they were looking at him."

PO-009 replied, "No. I would have to say not in all of the scenarios. I would say that I was treated unfairly in several of them…if not all of them."

PO-010 postulated, "No. No, I was not. Well, the, the jewelry store, for one thing…that's…it's the store proprietor, he can't expect to stay in business very long…treating people like that! It's ah…he, ah, that was not good at all. Ah, the hospital, we just saw…is people need to be treated better than that. Now, that's a foreign country, so they've got their own…problems, ah, and then I'm tryin' ta think of the other ones…the walkin' on the sidewalk with people rollin' up their windows…Yeah, that might not even be something they're doing on, like…not, I don't want to say on purpose, but it's almost like a reflex."

PO-011 added, "There were instances where I wasn't treated fairly. Um, some ones to me seemed blatant, um, ya know, in some of them, ya know, once you pick up on one blatant, then you start scrutinizing everything else."

PO-013 stated, "No. Ah, it really seemed that, in each scenario, it…each situation, typically are situations have gone from me in my past, I guess…um, and each one I felt singled out or avoided, I guess…specifically."

PO-014 concluded, "No. Um, I most, I dunno, I felt just depending on which one that you were…obviously treated different than how I normally am…so in my every day experience, there, I, like you said, I hardly have ever had anything happen to me, so it just felt like, um, yeah, it was different, just, automatically how they were, most people were treating me."

PO-017 was conflicted, "No. Ah, that's, that's a hard answer. 'Cuz again, my mind goes back to, is, is it coincidental? I mean…some, yes, some, no. Um, it's just, just what happens in today's society. Some, some of these things, I just, I believe it's just, it's just the way people are in general. Ya know? So, yes and no."

In summary, the majority of the participants felt they were not treated fairly in some of the scenarios. Each scenario had a different reaction from the participants. While one scenario the message was not received, another scenario drew upsetting emotions. Those varying emotions will be explained next. The inter-coder reliability for this theme was 97% agreement.

Theme Three: Wide ranging emotions felt

There were multiple different emotions felt through this experience. These participants did not have one major theme in the data. There were comments made about feeling angry, frustrated, and helpless. Another theme developed through the data of a feeling of privilege on the part of some participants. Each of these themes were reported in the data through the police participant's words.

PO-004 felt, "Pissed off. I mean, the ones where I felt like I was being judged, yeah, just pissed off."

PO-008 contended, "Ah, I was irritated with the one with the airport and with the hospital. I was irritated, especially with the airport one because it was targeted towards me. Ah, if I'm with this person at the hospital that, I don't know if it's both of us or for the person that's sick, that kinda irritated me."

PO-009 added, "Um, anger, some, but more just frustration because it didn't seem like it was warranted or even necessary."

PO-012 simply stated, "Frustration um, even anger sometimes."

PO-015 concluded, "Anger. Just 'cuz you could...I don't, you felt being singled out...and, ah, just being treated unfairly and just, makes, makes you angry."

There were more frustrated feelings among the participants.

PO-001 commented, "Frustration. There's definitely, ah, there's definite frustration within, in certain things and, and it had to do with, I dunno, immediately, I guess I'm lookin' at it like, oh, this...just...it's like...you wanna, I want to take it to another couple levels."

PO-002 added, "Maybe frustration for the person not sticking up for themselves and just leaving...and just like be done with it."

PO-009 stated, "Um, probably the most emotion was frustration, just frustrated that, ah, that I was being treated like that."

PO-013 concluded, "Ah...definitely frustrated, um, trying to run through them...frustrated, anger...um, that was probably the two most."

PO-020 contended, "Frustration...in most of those. It just...frustration of why and the repetitive and the continued actions of several repeat, that just...didn't seem like they were necessary."

There were also feelings of helplessness.

PO-010 contended, "It's like there's nothing I can do to change why they're acting this way around me. There's nothing I can do to change this. Pretty helpless. Pretty helpless. There's nothing you can do to change it...or change what they're perceiving, with these people around me are...perceiving."

PO-014 added, "Um, I felt helpless. Like you can't change who you are. So I mean, if they, it just felt like...if they already have this perception, then you're not gonna get out of that, just based, you know, you don't have a choice. It's like, it's already decided...in that, in all the scenarios, it's already decided how you'd be treated and you might be able to like, make a fuss about it, and things change, but it's not because they chose it, it's because you kind of, you made the fuss, you might make a scene, do somethin', so then they're like, oh, you know, we better take care of this...but otherwise, they probably would either ignore you or just...treat you different anyways, so."

There was an interesting dynamic drawn from this question. Although it was not specifically stated, the feeling of privilege emerged in the data.

PO-001 stated, "I don't know why anybody would sit through that. I mean, if they're gonna sit there and ask a thousand million questions, get out."

PO-002 added, "Well, stop complaining about it, get up, and do something about it and leave." PO-003 contends, "I'd go to another jewelry store, I wouldn't, ya know, I wouldn't put up with that."

PO-006 opined, "Instead of guessing why people are knuckleheads, listen, do you want, do you want my ID? Do I look like someone you're looking for? Do you want my ID, so you can check me for warrants?"

In summary, the participant's emotions were varied. Seven themes emerged from the data, however, eight participants mentioned the emotions of feeling angry or helpless, eight displayed the feeling of privilege, and nine were frustrated in the themes presented here. No emotion, confusion, and justifying the situations accounted for the other three themes, however, these only included between two and four participants each. The inter-coder reliability for this theme was 98% agreement.

Theme Four: Perceptions of the people in the scenarios

There were two primary themes in the data when the participants were asked about their perceptions of the people they encountered. The participants either thought the people acted inappropriately in some scenarios or the situations were justified in others. Eighteen of the participants mentioned the people were inappropriate.

PO-004 opines, "Um, majority, with the exception of the first one, the county fair where they were following me, ah, just rudeness. The county fair one was just...being jerked, I mean, just...over, I, I, yeah, I, that one was just way out of...line."

PO-008 pointed to a specific scenario, "I didn't like the airport scenario one, that guy was definitely was, ah...was targeting me for some reason. I didn't like that. The, ah, stern approach, I haven't, ya know, in my mind, I haven't done anything wrong, and I'm, I'm trying to follow these other people in, why are you pulling me aside?"

PO-009 postulates, "Like the restaurant, they could have been, ah, but and the last lady, the hospital, the clerk...the nurse, whatever she was...she, um, clearly didn't want to have anything to do with me and just putting me off or putting us off so…being rude, disrespectful."

PO-012 reflected, "Um, ah, rude. Arrogant. Um, I mean, I guess biased, ah, comes to mind. Um, I mean the people, the characters in all of these were, um, I guess, this, this was the first person thing…so, I guess it was just me in all of them that, yeah, you just felt, ah, I guess it'd be hard to go through your day not being, ah, upset all the time, ah, dealing with that frequently."

PO-014 felt, "That they were afraid or they, ya know, that, um, they interpreted as I'm different, not that I'm human, ya know? And so they just, um, treated me unfairly because, and didn't, ya know, I don't know how to explain it, I guess, but they, they treated me unfairly just based on…who I was around or what I was doing, um, without, ya know, just automatically maybe not thinking about it…it just seemed that way."

PO-015 summarized this way, "But for the most part, either avoiding me or making sure that I'm not doing something, um, yeah, I guess they're not…coming up, attacking me…or confronting me, but more…somewhat…trying to be subtle but not being so subtle."

PO-016 concluded, "Um, like the jewelry store one, you could tell that he was makin' a lot of assumptions about the…my friend, the female there…um…just by, just looking at her, and how she was dressed or her age and all that 'cuz he asked her a lot of questions that I didn't think were relevant to just looking at a ring. Um, I think that's the only one that I thought was a little much."

Other participants justified the people they encountered.

PO-001 stated, "I think, like, like I said earlier, just, um, that some of the situations were justified or just, ya know, um, circumstantial, we don't know the full story of everything that's going on." PO-003 contended, "Well, I felt that the one lady at the restaurant, ya know, they were very busy, so I don't know if it was an oversight? But I felt like she was very impatient as far as the friend I was with, and the other people were very busy, so I don't necessarily mean, think they were necessarily trying to avoid them. But maybe it was just an oversight on management or something."

PO-005 opined, "The customs screener and maybe the woman at the, um, doctor's office that obviously doesn't understand us and we obviously don't understand her. And quite honestly, that's on me. If I'm gonna visit a foreign country, I better be able to communicate a little bit."

PO-007 felt, "The scenarios didn't bother me, the situation I was in, the people I was with were more of a bother to me than the scenario because they were getting so wrapped up about something that…pretty easy to solve. Either walk away or, ah, or go ask somebody what the problem is."

PO-009 added, "The people…in the videos were not necessarily rude or disrespectful. I think they were just…either doing their job and maybe…not knowing the perceptions that they were giving to me. They were giving off."

PO-019 thought, "I mean, no one was overly helpful, I mean things could have…were made more difficult, um, for each scenario, um, than I have personally encountered. I mean, I've encountered difficulties but not to the extent of…these scenarios."

In summary, the participants were justifying some of the scenarios or found them inappropriate when it came to their encounters of the people in the scenarios. All of the other themes identified in this question had few common participant answers. The inter-coder reliability for this theme was 96% agreement.

Theme Five: Will you treat others differently?

The participants were asked if they would change how they treat others after experiencing their scenarios. The answers were nearly split down the middle. Twelve of the 20 participants made comments that this experience would not change how they treat others based on their belief that they already treat others well. Eleven participants made comments that they would treat others differently.

PO-002 commented, "No, 'cuz I mean, I know what is right and what's wrong…No because I try to do the right thing and I know that the bad people out there are gonna treat you wrong and then you leave and go somewhere else…so and I would of done that in the situations, it wouldn't change any, what they or I would of done…so."

PO-006 added, "No, I…I don't think so, um, I try to treat everyone with respect anyway."

PO-007 contended, "No, I don't think they'd changed how I will treat others. Um, maybe we all think this way, but I like to think I'm fairly fair to start with, so, um, I don't, I didn't see anything in there that would make me think that I would change my behavior from these scenarios."

PO-010 posited, "Well, I, I already treat people, no matter their skin color, as well as they will let me. Every time…ah…whoever I'm dealing with, it dic, they dictate how it's, how the interaction's gonna go."

PO-011 opined, "Ah, at this current stage of my life, no…'cuz I think I understand, at least a little bit…I can't say that, ah, I know how they feel, ah, but I, I can empathize and not, ah, know…when it's appropriate to, ah, when and how it's appropriate to talk and deal with certain situations. I also recognize that, ah, I mean, I, what I try to do is make sure that we don't participate in it, sometimes people are always gonna feel singled out…and, ah, so I just try to keep it as clinical as possible."

PO-016 added, "No, because I, I mean, I think I treat everyone fairly. So, I know, I dunno, I don't, I don't think it does, no."

PO-017 commented, "No. 'Cuz I…I…I'll continue to…I, 'cuz I don't treat people bad in the first place, so…it doesn't change anything for me…so."

PO-019 contended, "No, I don't think it'll change how I treat others. I think I try to be very helpful and, um, treat everyone the same, um, kind of already aware of that."

PO-020 postulated, "No, not necessarily because I feel that I try and I do, I feel I do a pretty good job of trying to respect each person that I come in contact with, regardless of the circumstance and that I deal with. I think it makes me more aware of some of that stuff that's goin' on that I never really thought about before, but I think overall, as far as how I treat people, I don't think that it would necessarily make a huge impact."

Other participants did think the experience changed how they will treat others.

PO-001 commented, "I'd say yes, 'cuz some things…I'll say yes because sometimes…I can't say it's, it's anything different…I, I'd say it's a reminder to say…for instance, ah, jewelry store, lots of follow up questions, lots of questionings and, um, and the reminder being is what I have seen in in my experience as a police officer, is telling people, following up with, explaining more situations with them,"

PO-003 stated, "Yeah, I think, as far as how I would treat others, is just, again, it helped me to take in perspective, as far as the African-American male...ya know, families are just walking across the street...but he may have encountered situations where that wasn't the case, they were trying to avoid him for a certain reason and if that was me, people were trying to avoid me... I see, I can see how that would negatively affect me...and when you're just... you're not doing anything wrong, you're just walking down the street...you just...um, so I think just trying to understand the culture or the pasts, the background...instead of just, don't look at it through a, a one lens glasses...look it, look at the entire picture. I think it's something, it helps me to...to take in consideration."

PO-008 opined, "I, on a regular basis, treat everyone well. Off duty and on duty. Ah, it's certainly an eye opener. Ya know? It's certainly an eye opener for me and it makes, and it makes me, I mean...it makes me more well aware, cautious when I'm with somebody who, who's a, a minority...ya know?"

PO-009 added, "Yeah, I would have to say some of the times...I would, some of the circumstances, if roles were reversed from here on out, I would probably take a look and make sure that I wasn't doing anything like that to offend somebody, er, to...put off that...to offend somebody. I mean, that's basically what it was, I was offended. Um, like I said, especially with the, the gentleman changing sides, that, that really irritated me more than anything. Um, and then ah, the lady, the clerk, just put off."

PO-010 posited, "I will, this has definitely opened my eyes to how, like, if I'm contacting an African-American person why they just flipped out. When I just say 'hey, somebody called 911, did you see what happened?' So, I could, and I already was aware of these...how African-Americans see themselves being treated, but now I have seen it first hand through these point of view videos, so, yeah, it changed my view...but I already treat people as well, as well as I can every time regardless, so."

In summary, the themes from this question were divided almost in half. Some participants felt these videos would not change how they treated others, while others stated it did open their eyes to a different perspective. In the perspective of these police officer participants, they already feel they treat people well. The inter-coder reliability for this theme was 97% agreement.

Theme Six: Can you better empathize with people who are treated differently?
The central theme of this research project was to see if cultural empathy can be changed through simulated experiences. When it came to the police officer participants, this question was asked. The answers showed 16 of the 20 had a positive answer to how these videos changed their perspective. To better understand these changes, one needs to look at the words of these participants.

PO-002 commented, "Yeah, I, I think so. I could, I could see, ah, how it can be frustrated to be treated unfairly. Um, 'cuz I never experienced something like the jewelry store, I mean, I've had some restaurant experiences like that or the customs experience, but if somebody's being treated unfairly, I can definitely see why they would want some answers or why they would want justification of why they were treated that certain way, for sure."

PO-004 contended, "I think, yes, I can empathize with 'em. I can, I do believe, yes. I do believe that, that gentleman, my buddy really thought that that family rolled up their window in the truck…I, I believe he thinks that they rolled them up because he was black. I think that he thinks that they crossed the street because of his race…Yeah, I, I, yes. How about that? So, long answer for a yes."

PO-007 opined, "Listening to my friend in the neighborhood and at the fair, I could empathize with the feelings that would cause him to verbalize what he is saying. I usually remove myself from the situation if I can…but if I can't, then I just deal with it. It's not, ya know, a problem, but getting a feel for, ya know, he's grown up his whole life with the feeling, whether it's right or wrong isn't the issue, but he has that feeling that people are looking at him and he's basing it on either race or on, ah, law enforcement, on the uniform. It may be something completely different, but I also don't know how you deal with that other than, like I said, communicating with them, talking to them. I can empathize with what he's saying, I may not agree with it, but I can empathize, I can see how that would cause him stress."

PO-008 contended, "Yeah, I can. The, the, ah, the neighborhood? The fair? Ah...the jewelry store? Ah, the, the hospital? Yeah, all of the scenarios were good. Except maybe the restaurant one because that one, I don't know what the deal was. Ya know, I don't know what their, their issue was."

PO-009 added, "Yeah, I would say so. I, I think I could...um...it brings to another light, I can't say that I haven't seen something like this before or similar to this before years ago. But it's good to have that refresher type to understand, ah, that, what it's like to be put off or be disrespected. I mean, that's really what it was. It was very disrespectful."

PO-010 postulated, "Oh, absolutely, and I have...I've even found myself on 911 calls, especially at stores with less than stellar private security...that, ah...I, I like the 911 calls where we get...ah, security calling in but then the person that they're, that security is calling about, calls 911, too...and first of all, you think, 'oh, this will be an easy one to take care of' and then I've actually empathized with African-Americans before on...yeah. I guess this guy's just one of 'em... sorry this happened...I've said that to people. 'Sorry this happened to you, but I'm not arresting you, you've done nothing wrong.' I mean, and then I even have to like, do a trespass warning thing, like, 'they don't want you at their establishment anymore so they, if you come back, you'll be arrested just for being here.' But...I...whenever I see that that happened to somebody, I, I'm sorry this has happened to you. I make a point to say that because...it sucks. It's shitty."

PO-011 declared, "I think it's a solid reminder, I think it's a good reminder, sometimes you can lose aspect, I would...I would hope at this stage of my life that I've, I've, ah, I've learned from my experiences and that I, ah, that racial bias training that we participate in annually is, ah, even helped to, just along with life experiences so...I'm not gonna say that I know it all, I can say that, ah, that yeah, this is helpful. It reinforces."

PO-012 argued, "Yes, and that's what I just addressed, I feel like, um, just, this feels like walkin' in, in their shoes...and, ah, the role players did a good job...they weren't goofin' off, they were, they were, they were genuine...and not likeable...when they're treating you that way, so that helps a lot."

PO-013 added, "Yeah, I mean, I can see how the...yes, I can better empathize with others because I can see how differently, they've been through different situations that...I've been through and had bring experiences with, yes."

PO-014 contended, "Yeah, definitely. Like I said, that's why it would add to the explanation of just, like, I get...um, it just opens your eyes, I wouldn't think half those things were wrong until...if, you've been around that every day, then they go okay...I see ya know, why you think that."

PO-015 posited, "Yes. Ah...you can see...I guess, um, a lot of things, I haven't experienced before. Now that I'm seeing research has been done on it, that it is prevalent, I can be more aware of it, um, and if I see things like that, I can either act on it or, um, at least better understand it."

PO-019 postulated, "Yeah, um, I think it's kind of surprising...um, ya know, I know that these are issues, like, I know they are issues, but they're not things that I personally have seen, um, I'm never really experienced people being treated differently. Like language, sometimes there's like some, there's barricades to how you can communicate with someone or how you can, ya know, understand how that person is going through, whether or not it's a different culture or language or just a different way they were raised, um, but I've never really seen people singled out and, um, being treated misfairly because of that."

PO-020 concluded, "I think I can. I can definitely understand, ah, some of the stuff that they may experience on a daily basis, just stuff that you don't necessarily think about."

Other participants did not think the experienced changed their thoughts.

PO-002 opined, "No. Because...I mean, 40-years-old, you know, some of these situations I've been through and, ah, there's bad people out there that treat you bad, so you move on and you go to the 99% of the people that don't treat you like that. Um, I would never say never 'cuz I don't believe in those. It's, it's possible that it could happen. But the fact that I've been to thousands of restaurants and I'm 40-years-old and never seen something like that, and I've been all over the country, and never seen an incident like that before, ah, where is...it was targeted due to race and not because it, being too busy and like, or whatever, I've never seen that where it's like 'oh, they're going to him because of his skin color."

PO-016 added, "I don't think it really changes my opinion." The inter-coder reliability for this theme was 97% agreement.

Discussion on what was learned

This research study was an experience in the life of another between two cultures that have had many historical problems in the United States. The researcher interviewed 22 African-American participants and 20 white police officer participants using seven pre-experience semi-structured questions to gauge their beliefs and six post-simulation semi-structured questions to see if their understanding of the other culture had changed. The interviews were analyzed for themes. The research established over-all themes of understanding another culture in a positive way. A total of 15 themes were deciphered in the data set showing common themes of how each culture views the other culture and how those views changed after a simulated experience of life in the other culture. Creswell (2013) contends there are two central questions that should be asked of participants. What have they experienced in terms of the phenomenon? What situations or contexts have affected their experiences in the phenomenon (p. 81)? The data in this study has highlighted these questions.

Most participants did not believe these things happen in the other's culture. For example, AA-015 had this recollection, "Ah, just because, ya know, the, they, ah, scenario with the broomstick? That was a direct threat, and ya know, with me not knowing the material of the broomstick that could have been something serious, ah, in retrospect, it would have been probably been better to mace them than shoot them, ah, and that's something that, ya know, law enforcement has to deal with and normally something like that would get blown up pretty big in the media."

PO-013 experienced empathy, "Yeah, I mean, I can see, how the...yes, I can better empathize with others because I can see how different, they've been through different situations that...I've been through and had bring experience with, yes." Each culture gained new knowledge and understanding into what the other experiences on a regular basis.

Discussion of the implications of the findings – their meaning and significance

Upon evaluating the literature review data to the data from this qualitative study, it can be argued that the findings of this research project were consistent with the data other scholars have reported. The majority of African-American participants initially in pre-simulation answers felt the police use too much force when dealing with African-American people. This feeling came primarily through word of mouth between people and not actual experience. However, once these participants experienced what it is like to have a use of force transpire in real time through simulation, the majority were surprised at how quickly things can go from bad to deadly force. Researchers have found similar findings in their studies (Schuck et al., 2008; Hurwitz and Peffley, 1997; & Broome, 2011).

Researchers have also reported through their studies that African-Americans are treated differently in their daily life interactions with people of other cultures (Brewster and Rushe, 2012; Dabney et al., 2006; Gardiner, 2000; & Anderson, 1999). Through pre-simulation answers, this was confirmed by African-American participants. Through post-simulation answers, this was learned and understood by many police officer participants. Surprisingly, these simulated videos were successful in creating this new understanding with experienced officers, which the data has shown are cynical and skeptical later in their career (Glomseth and Gottschalk, 2009).

Empathy through simulated exercises has been shown to be produced through experiencing another's culture (Kasl & Yorks, 2016; Klimmt et al., 2009; Vandsburger et al., 2010; & Patterson and Hulton, 2011). However, empathy was not tested in the data-set for police officers and African-Americans who experienced each other's culture through simulated experiences. This new data shows two distinctly different cultures whom have had many recent conflicts, can better understand their differences once they have experienced them firsthand through video simulation. Surprisingly through good video production, both cultures can gain new understanding of how the other experiences life and change the understanding they previously held.

The United States has a history of marginalizing ethnic groups of people. From slavery through the civil rights movement, African-Americans have been treated as a non-human or second-class citizen at best. Through Jim Crow and the Supreme Court decision of *Plessy v. Ferguson* making it legal to have "separate but equal" treatment of African-Americans (Sigelman & Welch, 1991, p. 18), African-Americans have always struggled for equal access and treatment. Media and early cartoons have portrayed African-Americans as having "ugly" (to whites) negative physical characteristics, such as distinctive hair, lips, skin, and odor (Feagin, 2013, p. 74). Today, African-Americans suffer the consequences of these generations of negative stereotypes that have held through time, although sometimes implicitly. Many white people do not understand what African-Americans encounter and must endure on a routine basis, thus little empathy is given to their plight from other citizens.

The police are the first line and easily accessible to the public as the face of the government. The police are sworn to protect and serve according to the constitution and the laws of the land. When the police have a use of force encounter, it is scrutinized by the public, media, and the police themselves. A police officer can be found guilty by the media and the public before the facts are even gathered and analyzed. A police officer who finds him/herself in the unfortunate position of having to pull the trigger in a deadly force situation will never be the same. If the person the force is used against is a minority, there is instant backlash, which sometimes leads to anger and protests. Use of force is not easy to understand, let alone to figure out in milliseconds. The general public typically does not understand this, thus causing little empathy from them when an officer makes a questionable deadly force decision.

This research study focused on gaining understanding and empathy from these two cultures in an attempt to gain new knowledge in ways we can bring these two together and create better relationships. Chen (2013) argues "acquiring another person's perspective" is essential in understanding empathy. First to become more empathic towards other cultures, we must understand who we are culturally. Then we need to realize the differences between the other culture and our own culture (p. 2267). Participants experienced how each culture faces challenges in their daily routine through simulated video scenarios. Important data was gained providing information that shows positive results from this study. The data shows a large percentage of both groups of participants developed understanding and empathy through their experience.

AA-016 exclaimed, "Yes. Uh, again, more empathy toward police, ah, hap, learning, what we see in the media or experience that have, of people using force more because of the seemingly aggressiveness of the...environment that they work in, the violence in the environment they work in."

While PO-014 contended, "Yeah, definitely. Like I said, that's why it would add to the explanation of just, like, I get...um, it just opens your eyes, I wouldn't think half those things were wrong until...if, you've been around that every day, then they go, okay...I see, ya know, why you think that."

When it came to pre-simulation interviews, both the African-American and police officer participants had mostly good things to say about the police and its administration. This can be partially attributed to a new chief of police arriving recently who is attempting to improve community relations. Peterson and Krivo (2010) argue there is a racial-spatial divide in this country that causes African-Americans to hold the least amount of power and the most disadvantage (p. 32). African-Americans participants in this study indicated Wichita Chief Ramsay has reached out to this community and understands their plight.

African-American participants felt by in large the police treat African-Americans disproportionately differently than their white counterparts. African-American participants also contended the police used too much force by a large majority (18 of 22). However, 15 of 22 participants stated they have never witnessed police abuse. Schuck et al. (2008) argue vicarious experience by people can be shaped through the exchange of observations and information about police interactions, creating an overall perception of the police (p. 500). Schuck et al. (2008) found through their study there is an important psychological link between feelings about the police and what is happening in people's neighborhoods (p. 515). Police participants felt they did not treat African-Americans any differently than other ethnicities. Police officer participants also were divided when it came to feelings on whether African-Americans commit more crime. Hurwitz and Peffley (1997) contended the disproportionate accounts of African-Americans related to crime are more likely to contribute to reinforcement of negative stereotyping of black people (p. 394).

While police participants contended they could remember a time when they felt they were treated differently, this study was more concerned with how African-Americans perceived being marginalized. Seventeen of 22 African-American participates stated they have experienced marginalization at some point in their lifetime. Some African-American participants commented on being treated differently in restaurants, stores, or in another place in time. In a study conducted with wait staff by Brewster and Rushe (2012), self-report questionnaires reported on average participants believed white tables were easier to wait on than black tables. Black tables were considered to be below average tippers in all cases, and 63% of the participants reported they over-heard coworkers and managers make racists comments on at least one occasion (p. 372). Dabney et al. (2006) found that despite intensive training and specific instructions to ignore shopper demographic characteristics, observers were unable to resist implicit cultural stereotypes in shaping their selection of potential shoplifters (p. 665-666). For these reasons, some African-Americans may have received poor services or more scrutiny in public settings.

When it came to developing better relationships between the police and the African-American cultures, both groups of participants had similar answers. African-American and police participants felt better communication and community policing efforts would help this relationship. Birzer (2008) reported participants felt the police needed cultural diversity skills, they should be good communicators, and officers should have human skills, such as sympathy, empathy, being personable, and being cordial (p. 204). Community policing depends on these humanistic traits.

In the post-scenario questions with African-American participants, 20 of 22 participants commented how difficult split-second decisions were to make in the simulated use of force scenarios. MacDonald et al. (2003) contended police officers rarely know what they will encounter when arriving on a call. Officers are required to make split-second decisions, which can be later viewed as unnecessary (p. 119-120). Broome (2011) found participants from a study on simulator use there was time distortion.

One participant in Broome's study stated, "Everything happened so quick, you don't get much time to think and make decisions." Participant AA-015 experienced the difficultly of split-second decision making as illustrated earlier in this chapter.

Broome (2011) contends if we really want to get the officer's perspective of what it is like to experience deadly force, there needs to be a methodology to analyze the subjective perspective (p. 140). African-American participants found not only split-second decision making difficult, but 13 of 22 participants had a change in feelings of police work. In this research study, the participants experienced six scenarios. Out of these scenarios, three scenarios required deadly force and three were non-deadly force scenarios. All of the 22 African-American participants were shot and neglected to shoot back at the suspects in at least one scenario. Jacobs and O'Brien (1998) contended the conventional assumption is police violence is a reaction to encountered violence, so police killings are a necessary response to the hostility they must control (p. 839).

This research study also found the suspect's ethnicity, according to the African-American participants, did not play a role in their decision to use force. Kochel et al. (2011) argue by merely demonstrating minorities are arrested solely on the suspect's race, other factors play into the decision to arrest, so confidence levels cannot hinge solely on the suspect's race (p. 476). Mastrofski (2011) posits it would be impossible to individually observe every interaction to determine the influence of the suspect's race on an officer's decision to arrest (p. 475).

The majority of the African-American participants felt the scenarios were realistic. Broome (2011) argued an emotional shock was experienced by all of the participants from being involved in the surprise attacks during the scenarios during this study (p. 151). However, this study fell short of measuring the psychological impacts of real-life police shootings (Broome, 2011, p. 154). Reaves (2016) found 99% of the U. S. police academies incorporated some form of reality-based use of force training. This training allows cadets to practice critical decision making, execute standard operating procedures, and under duress in real conditions employ potentially life-preserving tactics (p. 6).

The majority of the police participants also found their experience was realistic. Although simulated cultural scenarios experiencing another culture is rare in the research data, 17 of 20 participants stated this experience was realistic. These scenarios were based on the data which indicated African-Americans are treated differently. Anderson (1999) found when black people walk into stores, especially jewelry stores, they experience feeling disenfranchised (p. 17). Brewster and Rushe (2012) found wait staff treating African-Americans differently in restaurant settings. Gardiner (2000) found African-Americans received different treatment while traveling through airports in America (p. 1). Dabney et al. (2006) found implicit cultural bias in shaping their selection of potential shoplifters (p. 665-666). Each of the six police officer scenarios were based on these research studies.

The literature data set demonstrated African-Americans are treated differently than their white counterparts in certain situations. These white police officer participants experienced those feelings during the simulations. When asked if they felt they were treated poorly in these scenarios, all 20 police officer participants indicated they felt they were treated poorly in at least one of the scenarios. These police participants felt emotions of anger, frustration, and helplessness. Police officer participants also felt the actors in the scenarios were inappropriate, or in some cases, justified. Part of the perception of justification can be attributed to these participants finding solutions in their mind that they were unable to control due to the video simulation. Police participants also were divided when it came to treating others differently. There were 11 participants who stated they would treat others differently after their experience. There were also 12 participants who stated they already felt they treat others well, so this would not change their actions.

The central theme of this study was to see if cultural empathy could be achieved through simulated experiences of another culture. Acquiring another person's perspective is an essential part of defining empathy (Chen, 2013, p. 2267). Emotions shape our perceptions and what we believe and do. These feelings affect those we deal with in life (Goleman, 1998, p. 55). In this study, police participants were asked if they can better empathize with others after experiencing their scenarios. Out of the 20 participants, 16 stated they could empathize with others better after the experience. According to Chen (2013), we must see things from another's point of view to develop empathy (p. 2270).

Finding new ways of creating understanding and empathy between different cultures is necessary in this divided, decisive world we live in today. We must find ways to bring people together for common good instead of dividing us further and creating more hatred. This research attempted to find a new way to accomplish this. The words of the 42 participants speak for themselves. As the researcher, my goal was to show two different cultures what it is like to live in the other's culture. Their statements were based on the effectiveness of those simulated scenarios. It can be stated with fair certainty that simulated experiences of living in another culture is a safe way to experience who we are with positive results.

Essence

The essence of this study centered on the facilitation of simulating one's experience in another culture. Videos were used to allow the participants the opportunity to experience what it is like to traverse through the daily barriers which the other culture encounters. Police officer participants experienced through simulated videos what it felt like to be marginalized. African-American participants experienced how rapidly use of force can change through simulated experiences. Through this facilitation of simulation, participants experienced things they had not understood from their life experiences. Simulation can be seen as a modem of experiencing cultures through a different lens adding to the phenomenological method of research and the data.

Although the results from this research cannot be generalizable to either culture, the analysis and presentation of the themes provided the participants the opportunity to experience and better understand what it is like to traverse through the others' culture. The essence of the participant's experience of "walking in the other's shoes" through simulated situations allowed a safe environment for each to better understand struggles the other experiences. African-American participants were surprised at how quickly police calls for service can change and how difficult it is to make split-second decisions during use of force scenarios. White police participants had difficulty understanding why they were treated so poorly in their simulated experiences and gained more empathy for people who are treated poorly.

It is evident from these participant's willingness to take part in this study that they want to see this relationship get better. Both groups of participants felt better communication and more community policing would aid in this process. Both groups also appeared to gain new appreciation for each other once they experienced each other in a visual format. The powerful effect of visual stimulation was evident in the reactions during the simulation and the follow up questions with the participants. These experiences opened the participant's eyes to better understanding this dichotomy and the reasons behind it.

The unique approach of using simulation as a mode of experiencing another's culture was new to the data. These experiences were not absolute in effectiveness, however. There were participants in both groups who could not fully understand the experience and gave reasons to their beliefs that left them explaining away what happened to them. There developed a sense of privilege with some white police participants and the thought that training can erase the difficulty of all human error in use of force incidents with some African-American participants. Some participants were humbled at what the other experienced in their culture. The simulation had different effects on participants as one might expect.

Recommendations for Practice

Research is a valuable tool to create new and better training programs. Developing training that is capable of reaching human emotion is difficult to accomplish. When you take the oath to become a police officer, the true nature of this work is not realized. Police officers need to be psychologists, counselors, law enforcers, and solve a wide variety of people's problems on a daily basis. Police officers do not have the time during each call to truly understand the background of every citizen they come in contact with, nor understand their lived experiences. The problem on hand becomes the only essential thing the officer looks to solve, then continue to the next call. Giving police officers the training to understand cultural differences will allow them to better grasp underlining reasons for people's behaviors towards them. This research attempted to get two different cultures to better understand each other and gain more empathy for each other. Development of future police training around knowledge gained through this research study could help accomplish this.

African-American citizens have a limited knowledge of how fast use of force scenarios occur and change. Through simulation, participants gained new understanding of this. Police departments with simulator equipment could encourage citizens to experience use of force in a safe environment. Upon experiencing this better understanding between these two cultures and others could create collaborative relationships and less anger when critical incidents occur. This research study demonstrated how once people experience another culture, they gain new understanding of things they previously thought they understood or never experienced.

Colleges and universities have cultural courses designed to introduce students to people of other cultures. However, there are many areas of the United States where police officers are not mandated to get a college degree before joining the police force. These areas need in-service cultural training to better understand the differences between cultures. The colleges and universities which do have law enforcement or criminal justice programs should develop intensive courses designed to simulate experiences of living in another culture. Understanding other cultures through firsthand experience creates new understanding as this research study shows.

There are cultural conflicts in more careers than just law enforcement. Though police officers are authorized to use force on other citizens bringing unique critique, people in other career fields experience certain strains and conflict around cultural misunderstanding. These cultural misunderstandings may not become national headlines, they do have a strain nonetheless on the people experiencing them. Corporations around the country experience stresses due to cultural misconceptions. Development of cultural understanding training programs designed to best facilitate different occupations and ethnicity challenges are also necessary. There are many internal cultural misunderstandings between employees and various occupations which deal with individual interactions involving people of another less understood culture. Nurses, emergency medical personnel, human resources, correctional institutions, restaurants, stores, welfare departments, and government employees, to name a few, all have interactions with people of another culture on a daily basis, which is not well understood and sometimes misunderstood. New experiential simulated trainings around cultural understanding should be developed based on this research study.

This research project also paved the way for other simulated cultural experiences. Other cultures have similar experiences that are not understood between them and different cultures. Cultural understanding through simulation could be used in numerous organizations to create new knowledge, which are feeling the effects of cultural misunderstandings. New simulated scenarios could be developed to train expatriates on the culture of countries they are intending to relocate to better prepare them. Gianakos (2010) argues emotions are the universal language, which can help people bridge cultural differences and achieve mutual understanding and interpretations (p. 24).

Limitations of the study

There are several limitations to this research study. The first limitation is there were only 20 police participants and 22 African-American participants in this study. The experiences by these participants cannot be generalizations for all police officers or all African-Americans. Although the demographics and experiences of these participants ranged from 18-83, the average age of the African-American participants was 54.6 years of age. The average age of the police officers was 40.6 years of age with 16.2 years of service. How would a younger demographic effect the answers after the simulation experience? Would less experienced officers react differently? This research study took place in a large mid-western city setting. How would participants react in smaller or larger cities located in other parts of the country? This study also only included two cultures, African-Americans and white police officers. The results from a similar study with different cultures may not have the same effect on the participants. Upon reviewing the transcripts, it was learned three questions were never asked during the interviews due to researcher error. While it is not believed this would have changed the themes, it does weaken the data.

Another limitation to this study is the black community and the police officers who were interviewed had over-all positive things to say about each other. Wichita has not had an incident of police use of force on a minority that has made national news in recent time. If a similar study was done in a city that has experienced many police brutality accusations, would the data provide different results? If the African-American community did not like their police department as much as they appear to in Wichita, would the results change? If the police did not like their administration or felt they were not treated fairly from the public, would this change the data? These questions are hard to answer, however, it is apparent the relationship between the police and African-Americans in Wichita, Kansas appears to be better than other parts of the country.

Upon completing the research, the researcher thought more professionally done videos with paid actors who were more overt in their observations may have had a stronger impact on the white police officer participants. Giving the officer participants the opportunity to alter the course of the video also could have changed the participant's feelings of treatment within the simulation. Some participants felt frustrated or helpless to intervene and change what was occurring in each scenario they were viewing. Police officers by nature are wired to intervene and help those being mistreated. Giving the officers the ability to change the course of action may have produced different results. Upon reviewing the data, it occurred to the researcher the African-American participants were never asked directly if they gained empathy for police officers from their experience. Participants mentioned they gain empathy through other questions, however, a direct question could have produced rich data.

Finally, this research study and the literature review focused on the current issues between African-American males due to many highly publicized events, which have recently ignited this issue with Americans. The literature review did not make mention of incidents involving African-American females and the police. Although this issue is not inclusive to only black males, unarmed African-American males and the police has been the central theme to the issue in the media.

Future research

This dissertation showed common themes in how police officers and African-Americans think about their culture and the other culture. This dissertation also showed themes of how experiencing the other's culture through simulation can change how they think about the other's culture. Conducting interviews is an essential step in understanding how participants feel about their experiences. Future research could attempt to replicate this study in other parts of the country to see if similar or different results occur. Professional actors could be hired to add to the essence of the videos. New technology could be created to allow participants to change the course of actions they are witnessing in the videos. Developing more sophisticated videos with better capabilities for interaction could bring better results. Longitudinal studies could be done to determine if changes in beliefs continue or change with different life experiences of the participants.

In speaking with Doctor Lorie Fridell, it was learned that such new technology is possible and is being used by The Fair and Impartial Policing (FIP) team to train police officers around the country to better understand their implicit biases. "The FIP team joined with Will Interactive (WI) to create video-based simulation training resources. The resources were designed for individuals who have previously taken an in-class FIP course. The video training is designed to reinforce the FIP concepts/training at some point after the classroom training. The FIP student is placed into a video-produced situation in which an officer has to make a decision regarding what to do next. The video shows an officer or officers in the scene, but the student is supposed to make the decisions for those officer(s). At each step, the student will make a selection among options of what s/he will do next (multiple choice) and each option produces a different "next scene" that reflects the officer's choice. Key FIP training points/principles are inserted into the scenes. WI and FIP developed three such scenarios" (L. Fridell, personal communication, March 7, 2018).

New simulated scenarios developed around other occupational and organizational needs to understand other cultures should be developed, researched, and explored. Understandings between larger conflicts with cultures and countries could be explored to better understand each other and resolve their conflicts. Research studies between nationalities, ethnicities, and cultures in many settings could be researched and examined with the assistance of simulated experiences. There are conflicts and wars around the world which are started by cultural misunderstandings which could be researched with the assistance of simulated experiences. This study examined two cultures, however, new research studies could broaden this and examine multiple cultures through simulated experiences. There are many cultural conflicts around the world, both large and small, that could be researched and examined through simulated experiences to better understand each other. When it comes to cultural understanding through simulated experiences, the sky is the limit in where this can be utilized in research.

Understanding that women do not have it easy in this dichotomy, future research could also try to understand the effects of unnecessary police use of force with African-American females. This dichotomy is not solely between the police and African-American males. Further future research should look into whether or not older and more experienced officers are less empathic the more time they spend on the job. Research could also focus on whether police officers have a different association with understanding and empathy.

Future research could also focus on cultural responsiveness with the police in two forms: Development of culturally responsive training for the police, which shows successful results in practice, and researching new ways to develop more culturally responsive police officers. Vincent, Randall, Cartledge, Tobin, and Swain-Bradway (2011) suggest school districts add positive behavior support with training in cultural responsiveness to make it more effective (p. 219). This same theory can be applied to police training. This culturally responsive framework includes six culturally responsive practices. These practices are: (1) enhancing cultural knowledge (2) enhancing trainers cultural self-awareness (3) validating other cultures (4) increase cultural relevance (5) validating others' culture (6) emphasizing cultural equity (Vincent et al., 2011, p. 221-222). New knowledge into the police and cultural responsiveness through training could bridge this gap.

Definition of terms

African-American or Black. An American human being who has black African ancestors (Merriam-Webster, n.d.). For the purposes of this study, African-American or black will be used interchangeably based on their phenotype, not on individual ancestry.

Citizen Complaints. Formal complaints made to police departments about conduct which a member of the public has an issue with. Police departments will document the complaint and investigate the validity of the complaint. Formal investigations will be conducted for large scale complaints involving corruption and illegal activities.

Cultural Bias. Unreasonable opinions or hostile feelings towards a social group or different ethnicity, or age group (dictionary.com, n.d.).

Domestic. An incident that involves parties from the same household who engage in some type of altercation. A common term used in police work covering multiple altercations.

Empathy. The action of being aware, of understanding, being sensitive to, and vicariously experiencing the thoughts, feelings, and experience of another in either the past or present in an objectively explicit manner without having the feelings, thoughts, and experience fully communicated (Merriam-Webster, n.d.). Understanding another's lived experience to better see their perspective of how they interpret things.

Ethnicity. An ethnic quality or affiliation: a synonym to race.

Excessive Force. Excessive force occurs when a police officer uses more force than necessary to execute the arrest of an individual. Excessive use of force is based on what a reasonable person would believe to be necessary to take a suspect into custody based on the totality of the circumstances the officer was dealing with at the time.

Implicit Bias. The unconscious attitudes and beliefs, both positive and negative, held by an individual towards a group, person, or idea (Greenwald & Banaji, 1995, p. 5).

Institutional Bias. Unfair beliefs and actions taken against people by institutions such as the courts, government, landlords, and businesses, which negatively affects people in minority groups.

Institutional Capital. A term that is used when referring to minorities becoming needed personnel for farming, prison labor, and company growth, however the people are not available through traditional means so criminal charges are applied to imprison and staff needed laborers at little or no company expense.

Justified Use of Force. Force that is justified is determined through an internal investigation by a law enforcement agency or through the courts by judges and juries. Force that is justified by the police officer means a reasonable person believes the amount of force used on an individual during an arrest was reasonable under the circumstances.

Laser Shot Inc. A simulator manufacturing company located in Stafford, Texas that builds software and hardware which is used in simulation training in both government and public domains.

Mule. A term given to someone who knowing transports an illegal object or person for someone else.

Negro. *Anthropology.* (No longer in technical use) a member of the peoples traditionally classified as the Negro race, especially those who originate in sub-Saharan Africa. *Older Use: Often Offensive. A Black person* (Dictionary, n.d.).

Phenotype. The outward appearance of an organism: the expression of a genotype in the form of traits that can be seen and measured, such as hair or eye color (Dictionary, n.d.).

Police Officer. A licensed and sworn officer with the power to arrest and detain who is employed by a city, county, state, or federal agency.

Police Report. A formal document written by a police officer to document the facts of an incident. These reports are maintained within a data base which are accessible to the public for review.

Privilege. A right, immunity, or benefit enjoyed only by a person beyond the advantages of most. The principle or condition of enjoying special rights or immunities (Dictionary, n.d.)

Racial Profiling. Refers to the discriminatory practice by law enforcement officials of targeting individuals for suspicion of crime based on the individual's race, ethnicity, religion or national origin. (ACLU, n.d.).

Roll Call. Refers to a briefing done before each shift begins. Roll calls can be formal or informal depending on the agency. Usually facilitated by supervisors who detail events and information that has occurred in the recent past so officers are up-to-date with what is going on.

Security Officer. A uniformed person who does not have police authority or powers, and is employed by a private company.

Simulator. A device which represents or reproduces under test conditions phenomena which is likely to occur in actual settings which allows the operator to experience things through representations of events (Merriam-Webster, n.d.).

Suspect. A person who is believed to be involved in a crime by a police officer.

Use of Force. Use of force when applied to police officers can be anything as light as an escort hold to impact weapons such as batons, chemical spray, and the use of a taser. It can also include deadly force when applied to using a motor vehicle as a weapon to stop a confrontation and deploying a firearm by the officer.

White. A human being who has light skin tone European ancestry. For this study, the term white will be synonymous with Caucasian skin tone.

References

African American. (n.d.). In *Merriam-Webster's online dictionary*. Retrieved from http://www.merriam-webster.com/dictionary/african%20american

Alpert, G. P., & Smith, M. R. (1999). Police use-of-force data: where we are and where we should be going. *Police Quarterly, 2*(1), 57-78. doi:10.1177/109861119900200103

Alter, A. L., Stern, C., Granot, Y., & Balcetis, E. (2016). The "bad is black" effect: why people believe evildoers have darker skin than do-gooders. *Personality and Social Psychology Bulletin, 42*(12), 1653-1665. doi:10.1177/0146167216669123

Aman, A. C., & Greenhouse, C. J. (2014). Prison privatization and inmate labor in the global economy: reframing the debate over private prisons. *Fordham Urban Law Journal, 2*(1), 355-403.

Anderson, E. (1999). *Code of the street: decency, violence, and the moral life of the inner city.* New York, NY: W. W. Norton & Company, Inc.

Alexander, M. (2011). *The new jim crow.* New York, NY: The New Press.

Bachen, C. M., Hernandez-Ramos, P. F., & Raphael, C. (2012). Simulating real lives: promoting global empathy and interest in learning through simulation games. *Simulation & Learning, XX*(X), 1-24. doi:10.1177/1046878111432108

Banakou, D., Hanumanthu, P. D., & Slater, M. (2016). Virtual embodiment of white people in a black virtual body leads to a sustained reduction in their implicit racial bias. *Frontiers in Human Neuroscience, 10*(601). doi:10.3389/fnhum.2016.00601

Bayley, D. H., & Garofalo, J. (1989). The management of violence by police patrol officers. *Criminology, 27*(1), 1-25. doi:10.1111/j.1745-9125.1989.tb00861.x

Beckett, K. (2016). The uses and abuses of police discretion: toward harm reduction policing. *Harvard Law & Policy Review, 10*(1), 77-100.

Birzer, M. L. (2008). What makes a good police officer? phenomenological reflections from the african-american community. *Police Practice and Research, 9*(3), 199-212. doi:10.1080/15614260701797488

Blake, R. (1994). Diversity, common human needs and social welfare programs: an integrative teaching strategy. *Journal of Teaching in Social Work, 10*(1-2), 129-135. doi:10.1300/j067v10n01_08

Bolton, K., & Feagin, J. R. (2004). *Black in blue: african-american police officers and racism.* New York, NY: Routledge.

Brewster, Z. W., & Rusche, S. N. (2012). Quantitative evidence of the continuing significance of race: tableside racism in full-service restaurants. *Journal of Black Studies, 43*(4), 359-384. doi:10.1177/0021 934711433310

Broome, R. E., (2011). An empathetic psychological perspective of police deadly force training. *Journal of Phenomenological Psychology, 42*(1), 137-156. doi:10.1163/156916211X599735

Broome, R. E. (2014). A phenomenological psychological study of the police officer's lived experience of the use of deadly force. *Journal of Humanistic Psychology, 54*(2), 158-181. doi:10.1177/0022167813480850

Brunson, R. K. (2007). "Police don't like black people": african-american young men's accumulated police experiences. *Criminology & Public Policy, 6*(1), 71-102. doi:10.1111/j.1745-9133.2007.00423.x.

Buckler, K., & Unnever, J. D. (2008). Racial and ethnic perceptions of injustice: testing the core hypotheses of comparative conflict theory. *Journal of Criminal Justice, 36*(1), 270-278. doi:10.1016/j.jcrimjus .2008.04.008

Callanan, V. J., & Rosenberger, J. S. (2011). Media and public perceptions of the police: examining the impact of race and personal experience.

Policing & Society, 21(2), 167-189. doi:10.1080/10439463.2010.540655

Cancino, J. M., & Enriquez, R. (2004). A qualitative analysis of officer peer retaliation: preserving the police culture. *Policing: An International Journal of Police Strategies & Management, 27*(3), 320-340. doi:10.1108/13639510410553095

Carletta, J. (2008). Assessing agreement on classification tasks: the kappa statistic. *Computational Lingustics, 22*(2), 1-9.

Carr, P. J., Napolitano, L., & Keating, J. (2007). We never call the cops and here is why: a qualitative examination of legal cynicism in three philadelphia neighborhoods. *Criminology, 45*(2), 445-480. doi:10.1111/j.1745.9125.2007.00084.x.

Cassels, T. G., Chan, S., Chung, W., & Birch, S. A. J. (2010). The role of culture in affective empathy: cultural and bicultural differences. *Journal of Cognition and Culture, 10*(1), 309-326. doi:10.1163/156853710X531203

Chen, C. (2013). Empathy in language learning and its inspiration to the development of intercultural communicative competence. *Theory and Practice in Language Studies, 3*(12), 2267-2273. doi:10.4304/tpls.3.12.2267-2273

City of Wichita, Kansas (n.d.). Retrieved from http://www.wichita.gov/Government/Departments/WPD/Pages/Recruitment.aspx

Correll, J., Park, B., Judd, C. M., & Wittenbrink, B. (2002). The police officer's dilemma: using ethnicity to disambiguate potentially threatening individuals. *Journal of Personality and Social Psychology, 83*(6), 1314-1329. doi:10.1037//0022-3514.83.6.1314

Correll, J., Park, B., Judd, C. M., & Wittenbrink, B. (2007). The influence of stereotypes on decisions to shoot. *European Journal of Social Psychology, 37*(1), 1102-1117. doi:10.1002/ejsp.450

Correll, J., Park, B., Judd, C. M., Wittenbrink, B., Sadler, M. S., & Keesee, T. (2007). Across the thin blue line: police officers and racial bias in the decision to shoot. *Journal of Personality and Social Psychology, 92*(6), 1006-1023. doi:10.1037/0022-3514.92.6.1006

Correll, J., Urland, G. R., & Ito, T. A. (2006). Event-related potentials and the decision to shoot: the role of threat perception and cognitive control. *Journal of Experimental Social Psychology, 42*(1), 120-128. doi:10.1016/j.jesp.2005.02.006

Creswell, J. W. (2013). *Qualitative inquiry & research design*. Thousand Oaks, CA: Sage Publications Inc.

Crosby, J. R., & Monin, B. (2007). Failure to warn: how student race affects warnings of potential academic difficulty. *Journal of Experimental Social Psychology, 43*(1), 663-670. doi:10.1016/j.jesp.2006.06.007

Crutchfield, R. D., Skinner, M. L., Haggerty, K. P., McGlynn, A., & Catalano, R. F. (2012). Racial disparity in police contacts. *Race and Justice, 2*(3), 179-202. doi:10.1177/2153368712448063

Csikszentmihalyi, M. (1996). *Creativity. Flow and the Psychology of Discovery and Invention*. New York, NY: HarperCollins Publishers, Inc.

Cultural Bias. (n.d.). In *Dictionary.com*. Retrieved from http://www.dictionary.com/browse/culture?s=ts

Cush, I. K. (2013, December). Still not easy being an african-american. *New African*, 72-74.

Dabney, D. A., Dugan, L., Topalli, V., & Hollinger, R. C. (2006). The impact of implicit stereotyping on offender profiling. *Criminal Justice and Behavior, 33*(5), 646-674. doi:10.1177/0093854806288942

Dai, M., & Johnson, R. R. (2009). Is neighborhood context a confounder? exploring the effects of citizen race and neighborhood context on satisfaction with the police. *Policing: An International Journal of Police Strategies & Management, 32*(4), 595-612. doi:10.1108/13639510 911000722

Dempsey, J. S., & Forst, L. S. (2008). *An introduction to policing (4th ed.)*. Belmont, CA: Thompson Wadsworth.

Dovidio, J. F., & Gaertner, S. L. (2000). Aversive racism and selection decisions 1989 and 1999. *Psychological Science, 11*(4), 315-319. doi:10.1111/1467-9280.00262

Drexler-Dreis, J. (2014). Nat turner's rebellion as a process of conversion:

towards a deeper understanding of the christian conversion process. *Black Theology, 12*(3), 230-250. doi:10.1179/1476994814Z.000000000 37

Du Bois, W. E. B. (1903). *The souls of black folk*. Lexington, KY: Millennium Publications.

Durr, M. (2015). What is the difference between slave patrols and modern policing? institutional violence in a community of color. *Critical Sociology, 41*(6), 873-879. doi:10.1177/0896920515594766

Edwards, L. F. (2002). Status without rights: african americans and the tangled history of law and governance in the nineteenth-century U.S. south. *American Historical Review, 112*(2), 365-393. doi:10.1086/ahr. 112.2.365

Empathy. (n.d.). In *Merriam-Webster's online dictionary*. Retrieved from http://www.merriam-webster.com/dictionary/empathy

Entman, R. M. (1990). Modern racism and the images of blacks in local television news. *Critical Studies in Mass Communication, 7*(1), 332-345. doi:10.1080/15295039009360183

Ethnicity (n.d.). In *Merriam-Webster's online dictionary*. Retrieved from http://www.merriam-webster.com/dictionary/ethnicity

Feagin, J. R. (1991). The continuing significance of race: anti-black discrimination in public places. *American Sociological Review, 56*(1), 101-116. doi:10.2307/2095676

Feagin, J. R. (2013). *The white racial frame: Centuries of racial framing and counter-framing* (2nd ed.). New York, NY: Routledge.

Fraenkel, J. R., Wallen, N. E., & Hyun, H. H. (2012). *How to design and evaluate research in education (8th ed.)* New York, NY: McGraw-Hill.

Friedrich, R. J. (1980). Police use of force: individuals, situations, and organizations. *The Annals of the American Academy of Political and Social Science, 452*(1), 82-97. doi:10.1177/000271628045200109

Fullilove, M. T., & Wallace, R. (2011). Serial forced displacement in american cities, 1916-2010. *Journal of Urban Health: Bulletin of the New York Academy of Medicine, 88*(3), 381-389. doi:10.1007/s11524-011-9585-2

Furtado, V., & Vasconcelos (2006). A multiagent simulator for teaching police allocation. *AI Magazine, 27*(3), 63-74.

Gabbidon, S. L. (2003). Racial profiling by store clerks and security personnel in retail establishments: an exploration of "shopping while black". *Journal of Contemporary Criminal Justice, 19*(3), 345-364. doi:10.1177/1043986203254531

Gabbidon, S. L., & Higgins, G. E. (2007). Consumer racial profiling and perceived victimization: a phone survey of philadelphia area residents. *American Journal of Criminal Justice, 32*(1), 1-11. doi:10.1007/s12103-007-9019-6

Gardiner, B. (2000). Racism at the airports. *Network Journal, 7*(4), 1-3.

Glomseth, R., & Gottschalk, P. (2009). Police personnel cultures: a comparative study of counter terrorist and criminal investigative units. *Criminal Justice Studies, 22*(1), 3-15. doi:10.1080/14786010902796457

Goff, P. A., Eberhardt, J. L., Williams, M. J., & Jackson, M. C. (2008). Not yet human: implicit knowledge, historical dehumanization, and contemporary consequences. *Journal of Personality and Social Psychology, 94*(2), 292-306.

Goffe, L. (2011). The war that ended slavery in america...and blacks' part in it. *New African, 505*, 74-78.

Goleman, D. (1998). *Working with emotional intelligence.* New York, NY: Bantam Books.

Graham v. Connor, 490 U.S. 386 (1989).

Greenwald, A. G., & Banaji, M. R. (1995). Implicit social cognition: attitudes, self-esteem, and stereotypes. *Psychology Review, 102*(1), 4-27. doi:10.1037//0033-295x.102.1.4

Greenwald, A. G., Banaji, M. R., & Nosek, B. A. (2015). Statistically small effects on the implicit association test can have societally large effects. *Journal of Personality and Social Psychology, 108*(4), 553-561. doi: 10.1037/pspa0000016

Hagan, J. & Albonetti, C. (1982). Race, class, and the perception of criminal injustice in america. *American Journal of Sociology, 88*(2), 329-355. dio:10.1086/227674

Hall, A. V., Hall. E. V., & Perry, J. L. (2016). Black and blue: exploring racial bias and law enforcement in the killings of unarmed black male civilians. *American Psychology, 71*(3), 175-186. doi:10.1037/a0040109

Harris, D. R. (1999). Property values drop when blacks move in, because…: racial and socioeconomic determinants of neighborhood desirability. *American Sociological Review, 64*(3), 461-479. doi:10.2307/2657496

Heck, W. P. (1992). Police who snitch: deviant actors in a secret society. *Deviant Behavior, 13*(3), 253-270. 10.1080/01639625.1992.9967912

Henderson, M. L., Cullen, F. T., Cao, L., Browning, S. L., & Kopache, R. (1997). The impact of race on perceptions of criminal injustice. *Journal of Criminal Justice, 25*(6), 447-462. doi:10.1016/s0047-2352(97)00032-9

Hennink, M., Hutter, I., & Bailey, A. (2011). *Qualitative research methods.* Thousand Oaks, CA: Sage Publications Inc.

Higgins, G. E., & Gabbidon, S. L. (2009). Perceptions of consumer racial profiling and negative emotions: an exploratory study. *Criminal Justice and Behavior, 36*(1), 77-88. doi:10.1177/0093854808325686

Holmes, M. D. (2000). Minority threat and police brutality: determinants of civil rights criminal complaints in u.s. municipalities. *Criminology, 38*(2), 343-367. doi:10.1111/j.1745-9125.2000.tb00893.x

Hubal, R. C., Fishbein, D. H., Sheppard, M. S., Paschall, M. J., Eldreth, D. L., & Hyde, C. T. (2008). How do varied populations interact with embodied conversational agents? findings from inner-city adolescents and prisoners. *Computers in Human Behavior, 24*(3), 1104-1138. doi:10.1016/j.chb.2007.03.010

Hunt, R. J., & Swiggum, P. (2007). Being in another world: Transcultural student experiences using service learning with families who are homeless. *Journal of Transcultural Nursing, 18*(2), 167-174. doi:10.1177/1043659606298614

Hurwitz, J., & Peffley, M. (1997). Public perceptions of race and crime: the role of racial stereotypes. *American Journal of Political Science,*

41(2), 375-401. doi:10.2307/2111769

Ingram, J. R., Paoline III, E. A., & Terrill, W. (2013). A multilevel framework for understanding police culture: the role of the workgroup. *Criminology, 51*(2), 365-397. doi:10.1111/1745-9125.12009

Itkowitz, C. (2016). These black lives matters protesters planned a march. the police threw them a cookout instead. *The Washington Post*. Retrieved from https://www.washingtonpost.com/news/inspired-life/wp/2016/07/21/these-black-lives-matters-protesters-planned-a-march-the-police-threw-them-a-cookout-instead/

Jacobs, D., & O'Brien, R. M. (1998). The determinants of deadly force: a structural analysis of police violence. *American Journal of Sociology, 103*(4), 837-862. doi:10.1086/231291

James, L., Vila, B., & Daratha, K. (2013). Results from experimental trials testing participant responses to white, hispanic and black suspects in high-fidelity deadly force judgment and decision-making simulations. *Journal of Experimental Criminology, 9*(2), 189-212. doi:10.1007/s11292-012-9163-y

Jansen, B. (2016, July 17). 3 police officers fatally shot in baton rouge; dead suspect identified. *USA Today*. Retrieved from http://www.usatoday.com/story/news/2016/07/17/reports-baton-rouge-police-officers-shot/87218884/

Jefferis, E., Butcher, F., & Hanley, D. (2011). Measuring perceptions of police use of force. *Police Practice and Research, 12*(1), 81-96. doi:10.1080/15614263.2010.497656

Johnson, D. (2008). Racial prejudice, perceived injustice, and the black-white gap in punitive attitudes. *Journal of Criminal Justice, 36*(1), 198-206. doi:10.1016/j.jcrimjus.2008.02.009

Johnson, R. R. (2007). Race and police reliance on suspicious non-verbal cues. *Policing: An International Journal of Police Strategies & Management, 30*(2),, 277-290. doi:10.1108/014091704100784428

Jones, J. M. (2015, June 19). In u.s., confidence in police lowest in 22 years. *Gallup*. Retrieved from http://www.gallup.com/poll/183704/confidence-police-lowest-years.aspx?version=print

Kansas Law Enforcement Training Center (n.d.). Retrieved from http://www.kletc.org/bas7.php

Karimi, F., Shoichet, C. E., & Ellis, R. (2016, July 9). Dallas sniper attack: 5 officers killed, suspect identified. *CNN*. Retrieved from http://www.cnn.com/2016/07/08/us/philando-castile-alton-sterling-protests/

Karlsson, I., & Christianson, S. A. (2003). The phenomenology of traumatic experiences in police work. *Policing: An International Journal of Police Strategies & Management, 26*(3), 419-438. doi:10.1108/13639510310489476

Kasl, E., & Yorks, L. (2016). Do I really know you? do you really know me? empathy amid diversity in differing learning contexts. *Adult Education Quarterly, 66*(1), 3-20. doi:10.1177/0741713615606965

Kim, K. H., & Zabelina, D. (2015). Cultural bias in assessment: can creativity assessment help? *International Journal of Critical Pedagogy, 6*(2), 129-148.

Klimmt, C., Hefner, D., & Vorderer, P. (2009). The video game experience as "true" identification: a theory of enjoyable alterations of players' self-perception. *Communication Theory, 19*(1), 351-373. doi:10.1111/j.1468-2885.2009.01347.x

Klooster, W. (2014). Slave revolts, royal justice, and a ubiquitous rumor in the age of revolutions. *The William and Mary Quarterly, 71*(3), 401-424. doi:10.5309/willmaryquar.71.3.0401

Kochel, T. R., Wilson, D. B., & Mastrofski, S. D. (2011). Effects of suspect race on officers' arrest decisions. *Criminology, 49*(2), 473-512. doi:10.1111/j.1745-9125.2011.00230.x

Kurasaki, K. S. (2000). Intercoder reliability for validating conclusions drawn from open-ended interview data. *Field Methods, 12*(3), 179-194. doi:10.1177/1525822x0001200301

Kyles, P. L. (2008). Resistance and collaboration: political strategies within the afro-carolinian slave community, 1700-1750. *The Journal of African American History, 4 (1), 497-508.

Lee, W. (2016, July 10). For african-american police officers, a foot in two worlds. *Chicago Tribune*. Retrieved from http://www.chicagotribune .com/news/ct-african-american-officers-talk-about-crime-police- shootings-20160809-story.html

Levy, N. (2017). Implicit bias and moral responsibility: probing the data. *Philosophy and Phenomenological Research*, *XCIV*(1), 3-26. doi:10.1111/phpr.12352

Lytle, D. J. (2014). The effects of suspect characteristics on arrest: a meta- analysis. *Journal of Criminal Justice*, *42*(1), 589-597. doi:10.1016/ j.jcrimjus.2014.10.001

Ma, D. S., Correll, J., Wittenbrink, B., Bar-Anan, Y., Sriram, N., & Nosek, B. A. (2013). When fatigue turns deadly: the association between fa- tigue and racial bias in decision to shoot. *Basic and Applied Social Psy- chology*, *35*(1), 515-524. doi:10.1080/01973533.2013.840630

MacDonald, H. (2003). *Are cops racist?* Chicago, IL: Ivan R. Dee, Pub- lisher.

MacDonald, J. M., Manz, P. W., Alpert, G. P., & Dunham, R. G. (2003). Police use of force: examining the relationship between calls for serv- ice and the balance of police force and suspect resistance. *Journal of Criminal Justice*, *31*(1), 119-127. doi:10.1016/S0047-2352(02)

Madigan, T. (2001). *The burning: massacre, destruction, and the tulsa race riot of 1921*. New York, NY: Thomas Dunne Books.

Massey, D. S., Gross, A. B., & Shibuya (1994). Migration, segregation, and the geographic concentration of poverty. *American Sociological Re- view*, *59*(3). 425-445. doi:10.2307/2095942

Mastrofski, S. D., Reisig, M. D., & McCluskey, J. D. (2002). Police dis- respect toward the public: an encounter-based analysis. *Criminology*, *40*(3), 519-551. doi:10.1111/j.1745-9125.2002.tb00965.x

McLean, N., & Marshall, L. A. (2010). A front line police perspective of mental health issues and services. *Criminal Behaviour and Mental Health*, *20*, 62-71. doi:10.1002/cbm.756

Menzel, N., Willson, L. H., & Doolen, J. (2014). Effectiveness of a poverty simulation in second life: changing nursing student attitudes toward poor people. *International Journal of Nursing Education Scholarship, 11*(1), 1-7. doi:10.1515/ijnes-2013-0076

Merriam, S. B., *Caffarella*, R. S., & Baumgartner, L. M. (2007). *Learning in adulthood: a comprehensive guide (3rd ed.)*. San Francisco, CA: Jossey-Bass

Miller, A. H. (2001). The los angeles riots: a study in crisis paralysis. *Journal of Contingencies and Crisis Management, 9*(4), 189-199. doi:10.1111/14-5973.00169

Morrison, G. B. (2006). Police department and instructor perspectives on pre-service firearm and deadly force training. *Policing: An International Journal of Police Strategies & Management, 29*(2), 226-245. doi:10.1108/13639510610667646

Moustakas, C. (1994). *Phenomenological research methods*. Thousand Oaks, CA: Sage.

Negro. (n.d.). In *Dictionary.com*. Retrieved from http://www.dictionary.com/browse/negro?s=t

Nickols, S. Y., & Nielsen, R. B. (2011). "So many people are struggling": developing social empathy through poverty simulation. *Journal of Poverty, 15*(1), 22-42. doi:10.1080/10875549.2011.539400

Nowacki, J. S. (2015). Organizational-level police discretion: an application for police use of lethal force. *Crime and Delinquency, 61*(5), 643-668. doi:10.1177/0011128711421857

Patterson, N., & Hulton, L. J. (2011). Enhancing nursing students' understanding of poverty through simulation. *Public Health Nursing, 29*(2), 143-151. doi:10.1111/j.1525-1446.2011.00999.x

Peffley, M., & Hurwitz, J. (2010). *Justice in america: The separate realities of blacks and whites*. New York, NY: Cambridge University Press.

Peruche, B. M., & Plant, E. A. (2006). The correlates of law enforcement officers' automatic and controlled race-based responses to criminal suspects. *Basic and Applied Social Psychology, 28*(2), 193-199.

doi:10.1207/s15324834basp2802_9

Peterson, R. D., & Krivo, L. J. (2010). *Divergent social worlds: neighborhood crime and the racial-spatial divide*. New York, NY: Russell Sage Foundation.

Petrocelli, M., Piquero, A. R., & Smith, M. R. (2002). Conflict theory and racial profiling: an empirical analysis of police traffic stop data. *Journal of Criminal Justice, 31*(1), 1-11. doi:10.1016/s0047-2352(02)00195-2

Phenotype. (n.d.). In *The American Heritage New Dictionary of Cultural Literacy* (3rd ed.). Retrieved from http://www.dictionary.com/browse/phenotype

Plant, E. A., Peruche, B. M. (2005). The consequences of race for police officers responses to criminal suspects. *Psychological Science, 16*(3), 180-183. doi:10.1111/j.0956-7976.2005.00800.x

Plant. E. A., Peruche, B. M., & Butz, D. A. (2005). Eliminating automatic racial bias: making race non-diagnostic for responses to criminal suspects. *Journal of Experimental Social Psychology, 41*(1), 141-156. doi:10.1016/j.jesp.2004.07.004

Pollak, L. H. (2005). Race, law, and history: the supreme court from "dred scott" to "grutter v. bollinger". *Daedalus, 134*(1), 29-41. doi:10.1162/0011526053124488

Privilege. (n.d.). In *Dictionary.com*. Retrieved from http://www.dictionary.com/browse/privilege

Quillian, L., & Pager, D. (2001). Black neighbors, higher crime? The role of racial stereotypes in evaluations of neighborhood crime. *American Journal of Sociology, 107*(3), 717-767. doi:10.1086/338938

Racial profiling. (n.d.). In *ACLU's online definition*. Retrieved from https://www.aclu.org/racial-profiling-definition

Reaves, B. A. (2016). *State and local law enforcement training academies, 2013. U.S. Department of Justice*. Washington: Bureau of Justice Statistics.

Renauer, B. C., & Covelli, E. (2010). Examining the relationship between police experiences and perceptions of police bias. *Policing: An International Journal of Police Strategies & Management, 34*(3), 497-514.

doi:10.1108/13639511111157537

Rogoeczi, W. C., & Kent, S. (2014). Race, poverty, and the traffic ticket cycle: exploring the situational context of the application of police discretion. *Policing: An International Journal of Police Strategies & Management, 37*(1), 190-205. doi:10.1108/PIJPSM-06-2013-0060

Sarkis, J. (2012). Editorial: Models for compassionate operations. *International Journal of Production Economics, 139*(1), 359-365. doi:10.1016/j.ipe.2012.06.018

Schuck, A., & Martin, C. (2013). Residents' perceptions of procedural injustice during encounters with the police. *Journal of Ethnicity in Criminal Justice, 11*(1), 219-237. doi:10.1080/15377938.2012.762635

Schuck, A. M., Rosenbaum, D. P., & Hawkins, D. F. (2008). The influence of race/ethnicity, social class, and neighborhood context on residents' attitudes toward the police. *Police Quarterly, 11*(4), 496-519. doi:10.1177/1098611108318115

Schulenberg, J. L. (2015). Moving beyond arrest and conceptualizing police discretion: an investigation into the factors affecting conversation, assistance, and criminal charges. *Police Quarterly, 18*(3), 244-271. doi:10.1177/1098611115577144

Segal, E. A. (2007). Social empathy: a new paradigm to address poverty. *Journal of Poverty, 11*(3), 65-81. doi:10.1300/J134v11n03_06

Shapiro, J., & Gianakos, D. (2010, January). Teaching through movies in a multicultural scenario: overcoming cultural barriers through emotions and reflection. *Family Medicine, 42*(1), 22-24

Sigelman, L. & Welch, S. (1991). *Black americans' views of racial inequity: The dream deferred.* New York, NY: Cambridge University Press.

Simulator. (n.d.). *Merriam-Webster's online dictionary.* Retrieved from http://www.merriam-webster.com/dictionary/simulator

Smith, B. W., & Holmes, M. D. (2003). Community accountability, minority threat, and police brutality: an examination of civil rights criminal complaints. *Criminology, 41*(4), 1035-1063. doi:10.1111/j.1745-9125.2003.tb01013.x

Soto, J. A., & Levenson, R. W. (2009). Emotion recognition across cultures: the influence of ethnicity on empathic accuracy and physiological linkage. *Emotion, 9*(6), 874-884. doi:10.1037/a0017399

South, S. J., & Crowder, K. D. (1998). Leaving the 'hood: residential mobility between black, white, and integrated neighborhoods. *American Sociological Review, 63*(1), 17-26. doi:10.2307/2657474

Stewart, E. A., Baumer, E. P., Brunson, R. K., & Simons, R. L. (2009). Neighborhood racial context and perceptions of police-based racial discrimination among black. *Criminology, 47*(3), 847-887. doi:10.1111/j.1745-9125.2009.00159.x.

Stewart, J. B. (1995). Race, science, and "just-us": understanding jurors' reasonable doubt in the OJ Simpson trial. *The Black Scholar, 25*(4), 43-45.

Tennenbaum, A. N. (1994). The influence of the garner decision on police use of deadly force. *The Journal of Criminal Law & Criminology, 85*(1), 241-260. doi:10.2307/1144118

Tennessee v. Garner, 471 U.S. 1 (1985).

Terrill, W. (2003). Police use of force and suspect resistance: the micro process of the police-suspect encounter. *Police Quarterly, 6*(1), 51-83. doi:10.1177/1098611102250584

Terrill, W., & Paoline, E. A. (2012). Examining less lethal force policy and the force continuum: results from a national use-of-force study. *Police Quarterly, 16*(1), 38-65. doi:10.1177/1098611112451262

Terrill, W., & Reisig, M. (2003). Neighborhood context and police use of force. *Journal of Research in Crime and Delinquency, 40*(3), 291-321. doi:10.1177/0022427803253800

Thornton, J. K. (1991). African dimensions of the stono rebellion. *American Historical Review, 96*(4), 1101-1113. doi:10.2307/2164997

Turner, K. B., Giacopassi, D., & Vandiver, M. (2006). Ignoring the past: coverage of slavery and slave patrols in criminal justice texts. *Journal of Criminal Justice Education, 17*(1), 182-195. doi:10.1080/10511250500335627

United States Department of Justice, Civil Rights Division. (2015). *Investigation of the ferguson police department*. Retrieved from http://www.justice.gov/.../ferguson_police_...

Vandsburger, E., Duncan-Daston, R., Akerson, E., & Dillon, T. (2010). The effects of poverty simulation, an experiential learning modality, on students' understanding of life in poverty. *Journal of Teaching in Social Work, 30*(3), 300-316. doi:10.1080/08841233.2010.497129

Vincent, C. G., Randall, C., Cartledge, G., Tobin, T. J., & Swain-Bradway, J. (2011). Towards a conceptual integration of cultural responsiveness and schoolwide positive behavior support. *Journal of Positive Behavior Interventions, 13*(4), 219-229. doi:10.1177/1098300711399765

Waddington, P. A. J. (1999). Police (canteen) sub-culture. *British Journal of Criminology, 39*(2), 287-309. doi:10.1093/bjc/39.2.287

Walker, S. (1998). *Popular justice: a history of american criminal justice* (2nd ed.). New York, NY: Oxford University Press.

Washington, B. T. (1911). The Negro in the new world. *Journal of the Royal African Society, 10*(38), 173-178.

Washington, B. T. (1910). The Negro's part in southern development. *The Annals of the American Academy of Political and Social Science, 35*(1), 124-133. doi:10.1177/000271621003500116

Washington, B. T. (1912). The rural negro community. *The Annals of the American Academy of Political and Social Science, 40*(1), 81-89. doi:10.1177/000271621204000111

Wehrman, M. M., & De Angelis, J. (2011). Citizen willingness to participate in police-community partnerships: exploring the influence of race and neighborhood context. *Police Quarterly, 14*(1), 48-69. doi:10.1177/1098611110393134

Weitzer, R. (2002). Incidents of police misconduct and public opinion. *Journal of Criminal Justice, 30*(1), 397-408. doi:10.1016/S0047-2352(02)00150-2

Weitzer, R., & Tuch, S. A. (1999). Race, class, and perceptions of discrimination by the police. *Crime & Delinquency, 45*(4), 494-507. doi:10.11

77/0011128799045004006

Weitzer, R., & Tuch, S. A (2002). Perceptions of racial profiling: race, class, and personal experience. *Criminology, 40*(2), 435-456.doi:10.1111/j.1745-9125.2002.tb00962.x

White, C. R., Carson, J. L., & Wilbourn, J. M. (1991). Training effectiveness of an m-16 rifle simulator. *Military Psychology, 3*(3), 177-184. doi:10.1207/s153278876mp0303_4

Wichita City, Kansas (2010). *United States Census Bureau*. Retrieved from http://www.census.gov/quickfacts/table/PST045215/2079000

Wichita Police Department Policy Manual, Regulation 4.0 – Weapons/Use of Force Requirements (2013). Retrieved from http://www.wichita.gov/Government/Departments/WPD/Pages/Pol icy.aspx

Woods, L. L. (2012). The federal home loan bank board, redlining, and the national proliferation of racial lending discrimination, 1921-1950. *Journal of Urban Study, 38*(6), 1036-1059.doi:10.1177/00 96144211435126

Yin, R. K. (2011). *Qualitative research from start to finish*. New York, NY: The Guilford Press.

Zeisel, H. (1981). Race bias in the administration of the death penalty: the florida experience.*Harvard Law Review, 95*(2), 455-468. doi:10.2307 /1340711

www.ingramcontent.com/pod-product-compliance
Lightning Source LLC
Chambersburg PA
CBHW070646290526
45790CB00001B/197